The White Stripes
ELEPHANT

Transcribed by Steve Gorenberg

Album artwork by The Third Man
Album layout by Bruce Brand at Arthole
White Stripes photography by Patrick Pantano

ISBN 978-1-57560-681-1

Visit our website at www.cherrylane.com

Contents

SEVEN NATION ARMY

Words and Music by
Jack White

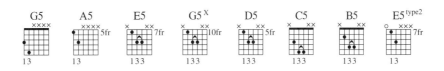

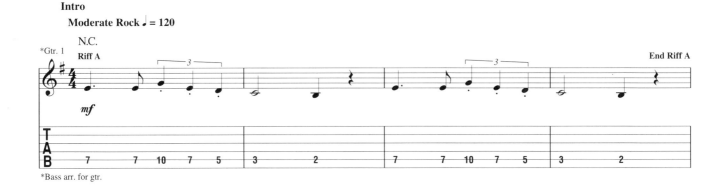

Intro

Moderate Rock ♩ = 120

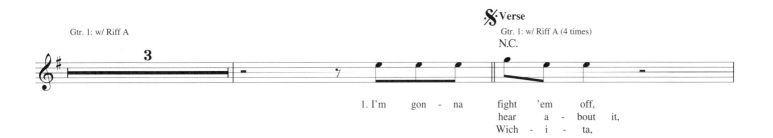

*Bass arr. for gtr.

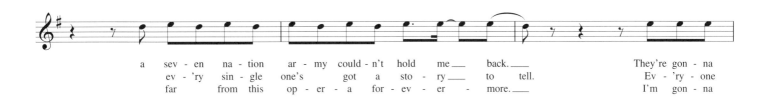

1. I'm gon-na fight 'em off,
hear a-bout it,
Wich - i - ta,

a sev-en na-tion ar-my could-n't hold me ___ back. ___ They're gon-na
ev-'ry sin-gle one's got a sto-ry ___ to tell. ___ Ev-'ry-one
far from this op-er-a for-ev-er-more. ___ I'm gon-na

rip it off,   tak-ing their time right be-hind my ___ back. ___
knows a-bout it,   from the Queen of Eng-land to the hounds of ___ hell. ___
work the straw,   make the sweat drip out of ev-'ry ___ pore. ___

___   And I'm talk-ing to my-self at ___ night ___ be-cause I can't for-get. ___
___   And if I catch it com-ing back my ___ way I'm gon-na serve it to you. ___
___   And I'm bleed-ing, and I'm bleed-ing, and I'm bleed-ing right be-fore the ___ Lord. ___

3

Back and forth through my _____ mind ___
And that ain't what you want to _____ hear, ___
All the words are gon - na bleed from _____ me ___

___ be - hind a cig - a - rette. _____
___ but that's what I'll ___ do. _____
___ and I will think no ___ more. _____ And the
And the
And the

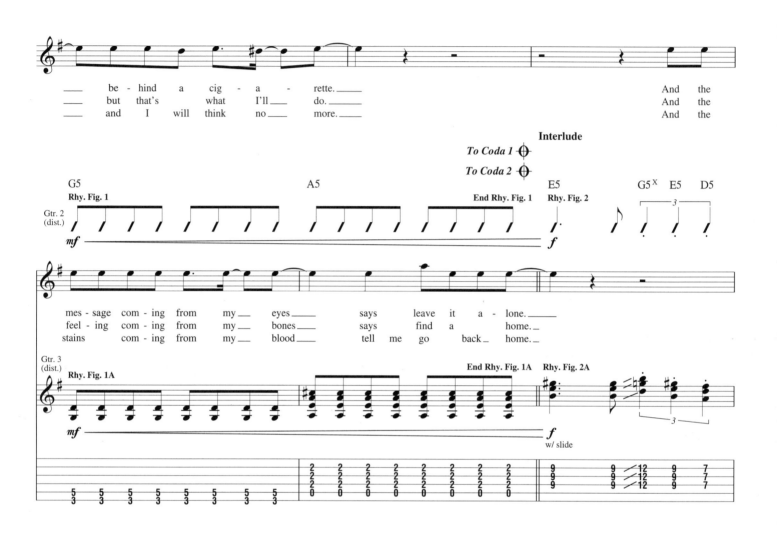

Interlude

To Coda 1 ⊕
To Coda 2 ⊕

G5   A5   E5   G5ˣ E5 D5

Rhy. Fig. 1   End Rhy. Fig. 1   Rhy. Fig. 2
Gtr. 2 (dist.)
mf   *f*

mes - sage com - ing from my ___ eyes ___ says leave it a - lone. ___
feel - ing com - ing from my ___ bones ___ says find a home. ___
stains com - ing from my ___ blood ___ tell me go back _ home. ___

Gtr. 3 (dist.)   End Rhy. Fig. 1A   Rhy. Fig. 2A
Rhy. Fig. 1A
mf   *f*
w/ slide

Gtrs. 2 & 3: w/ Rhy. Figs. 2 & 2A
C5   B5   E5   G5ˣ E5 D5   C5 D5 C5 B5   E   G E D
                                        End Rhy. Fig. 2

End Rhy. Fig. 2A

Gtrs. 2 & 3: w/ Rhy. Figs. 1 & 1A
C   B   E   G E D C D C B   A/B   G5

2. Don't wan - na

⊕ Coda 1

Guitar Solo

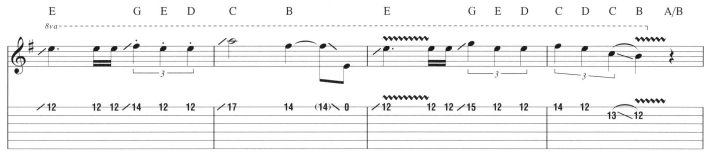

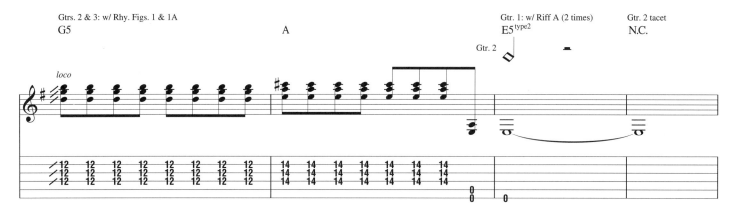

D.S. al Coda 2

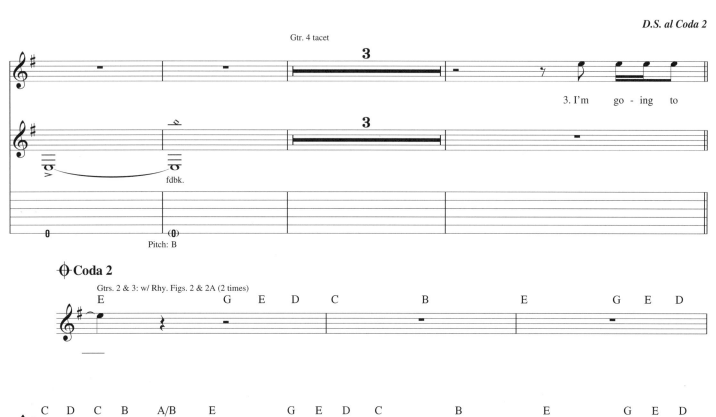

3. I'm go - ing to

Pitch: B

⊕ Coda 2

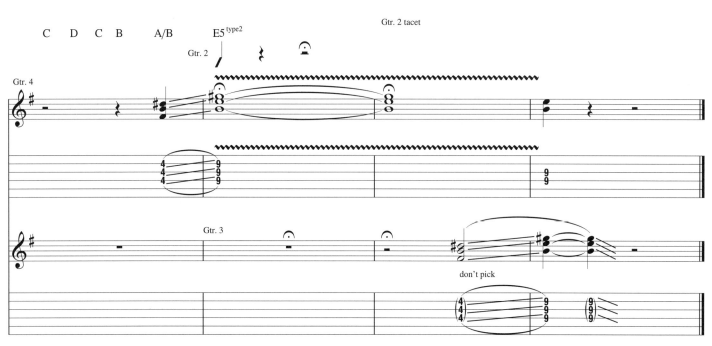

don't pick

BLACK MATH

Words and Music by
Jack White

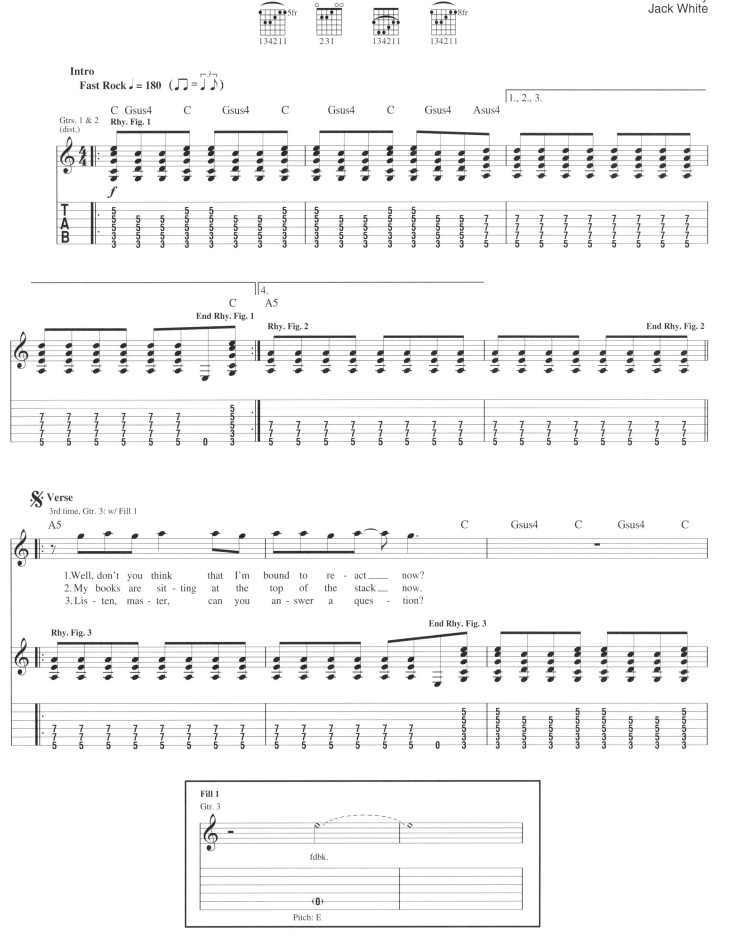

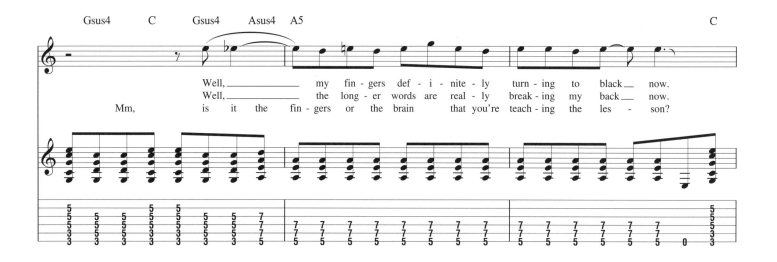

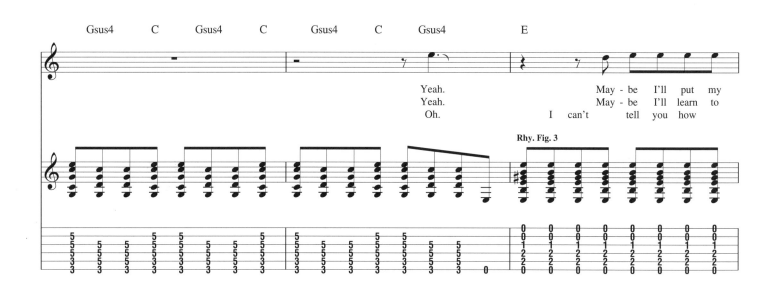

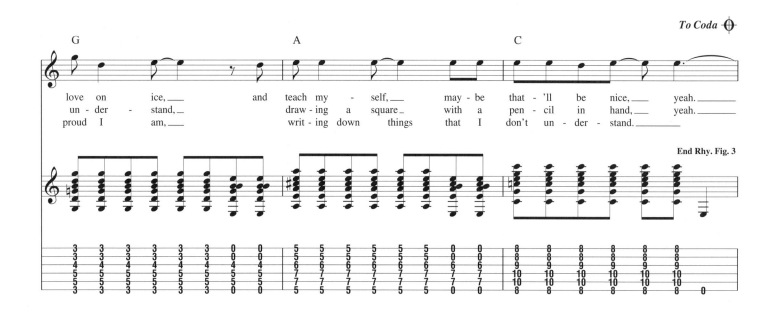

Gtrs. 1 & 2: w/ Rhy. Fig. 2 (2 times)

*Flick toggle switch on and off in rhythm indicated.

9

Coda

Well, may-be _____ I'll put my love on ice _____ and teach my-self. _____ May-be that 'll be nice, _____ yeah. _____

Outro

_____ Yeah. Yeah.

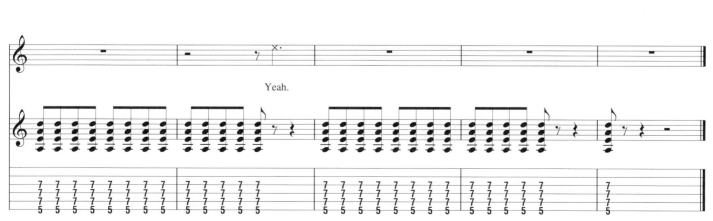

Yeah.

THERE'S NO HOME FOR YOU HERE

Words and Music by
Jack White

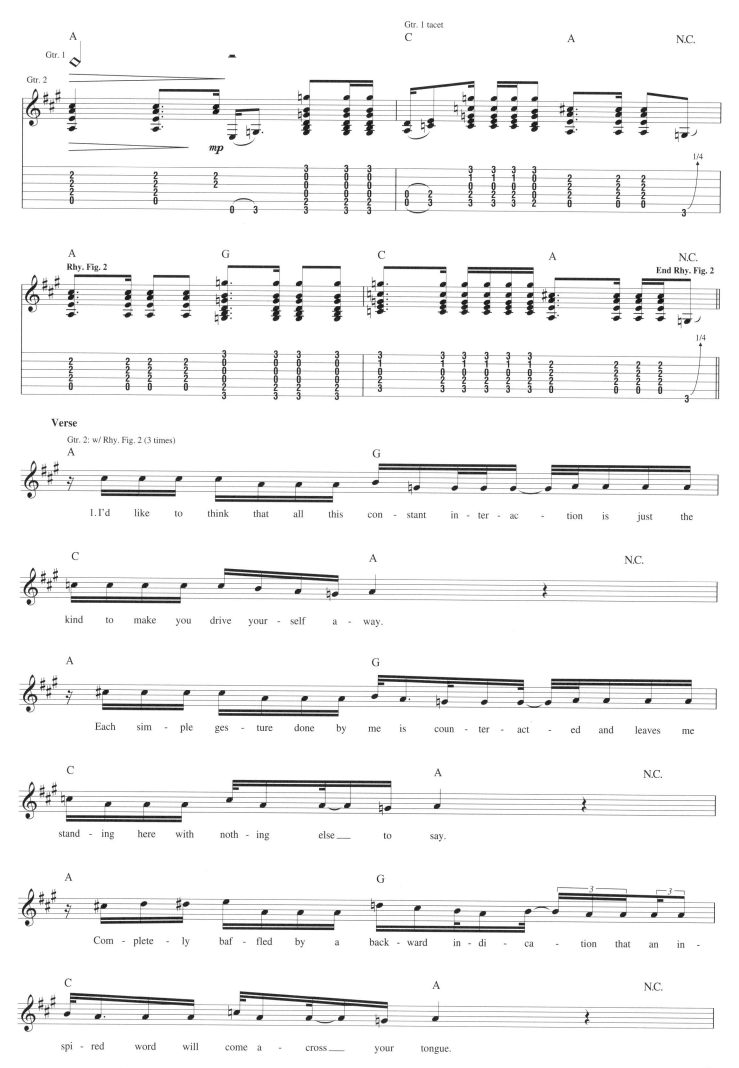

Verse

1. I'd like to think that all this con-stant in-ter-ac-tion is just the kind to make you drive your-self a-way.

Each sim-ple ges-ture done by me is coun-ter-act-ed and leaves me stand-ing here with noth-ing else____ to say.

Com-plete-ly baf-fled by a back-ward in-di-ca-tion that an in-spi-red word will come a-cross____ your tongue.

A   G

Hands mov - ing up - ward to pro - pel___ the sit - u - a - tion have sim - ply

Gtr. 2

C   A   G

halt - ed, now the con - ver - sa - tion's___ done.

Gtr. 1

f

Gtr. 2

f

1/4

Chorus

Gtrs. 1 & 2: w/ Rhy. Fig. 1

A   G   C   A   G

There's no home for you here, girl; go a - way.   There's no home for you here.

Gtr. 1 tacet

A   C   A   G

Gtr. 1

Gtr. 2

mp

1/4

14

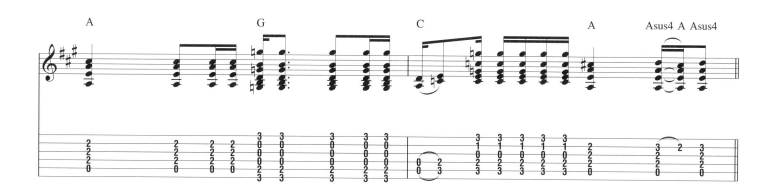

Verse

Gtr. 2: w/ Rhy. Fig. 2 (3 times)

2. I'm on - ly wait - ing for the prop - er time to tell you that it's im - pos - si - ble to get a - long with you.

It's hard to look you in the face when we are talk - ing, so it helps to have a mir - ror in the room.

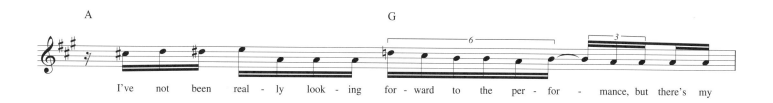

I've not been real - ly look - ing for - ward to the per - for - mance, but there's my

cue and there's a ques - tion on your face.

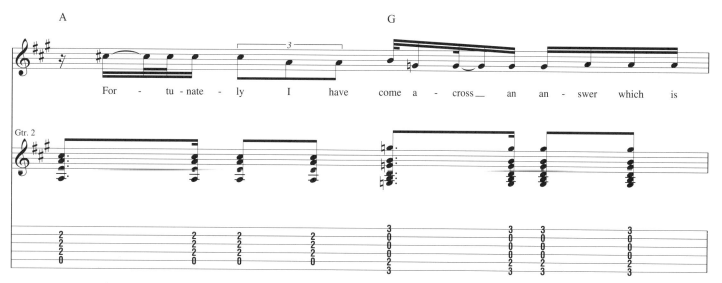

For - tu - nate - ly I have come a - cross an an - swer which is

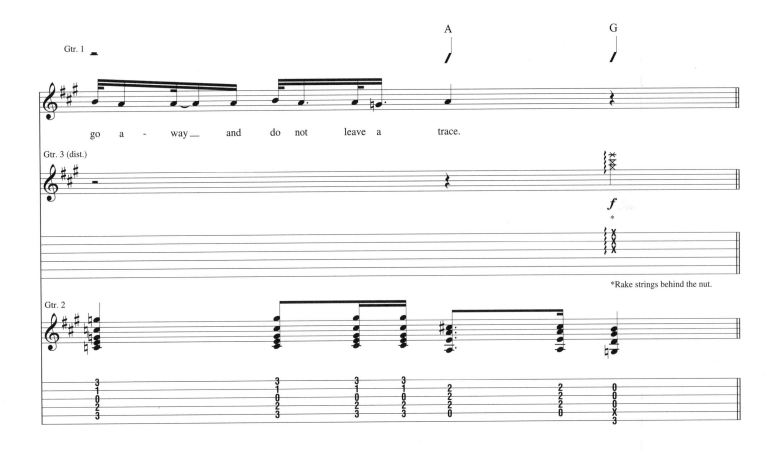

go a - way___ and do not leave a trace.

*Rake strings behind the nut.

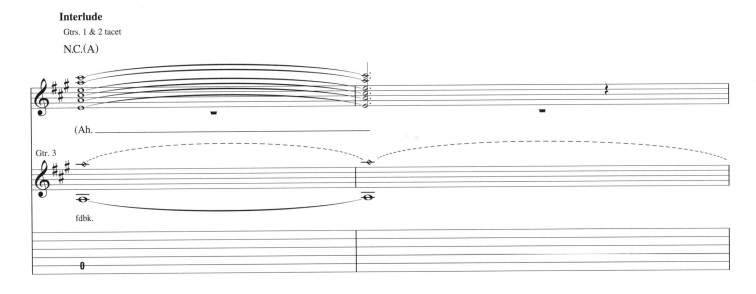

Interlude

Gtrs. 1 & 2 tacet

N.C.(A)

(Ah. _____

fdbk.

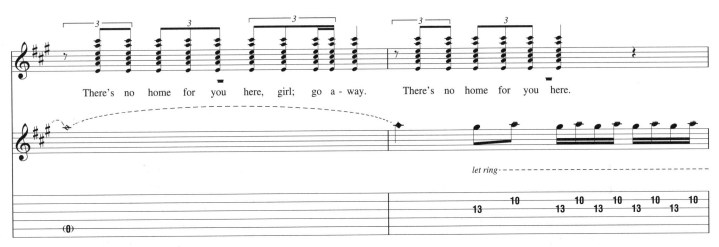

There's no home for you here, girl; go a - way. There's no home for you here.

let ring -

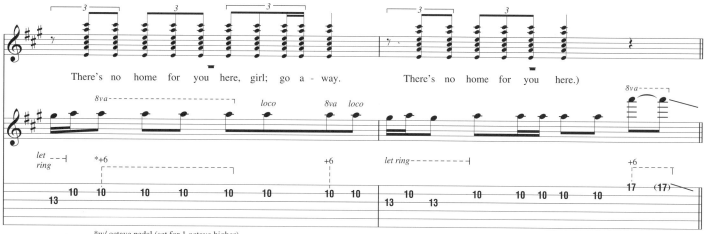

There's no home for you here, girl; go a - way.   There's no home for you here.)

*w/ octave pedal (set for 1 octave higher)

Guitar Solo

Gtrs. 1 & 2: w/ Rhy. Fig. 1 (2 times)

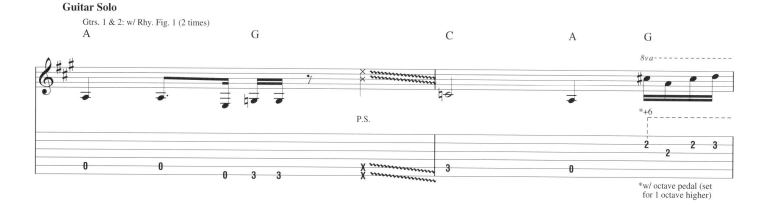

*w/ octave pedal (set for 1 octave higher)

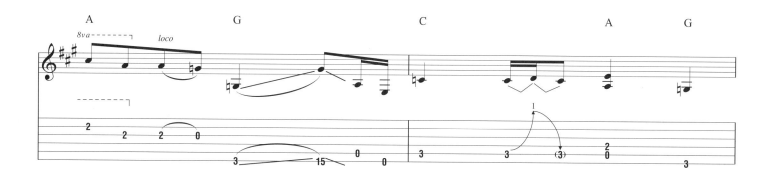

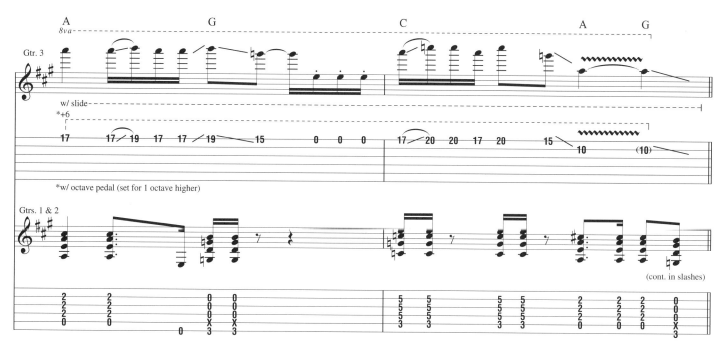

(cont. in slashes)

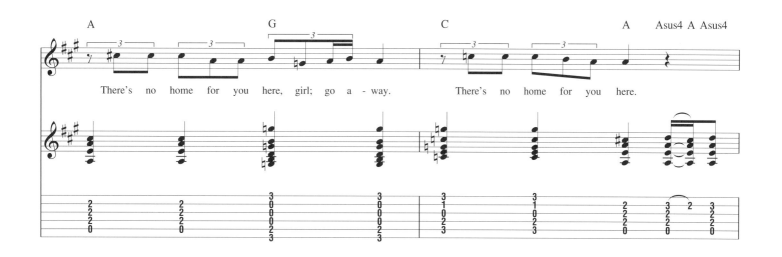

There's no home for you here, girl; go a-way. There's no home for you here.

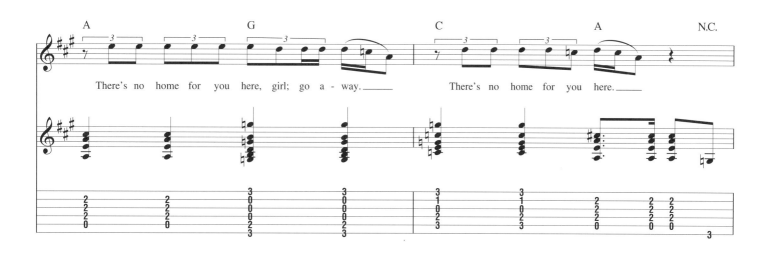

There's no home for you here, girl; go a-way._____ There's no home for you here._____

There's no home for you here, girl; go a-way. No home_____ here._____

Outro

Gtrs. 1 & 2: w/ Rhy. Fig. 1

Repeat and fade

There's no home for you here, girl; go a-way. There's no home for you here.

I JUST DON'T KNOW WHAT TO DO WITH MYSELF

Lyric by Hal David
Music by Burt Bacharach

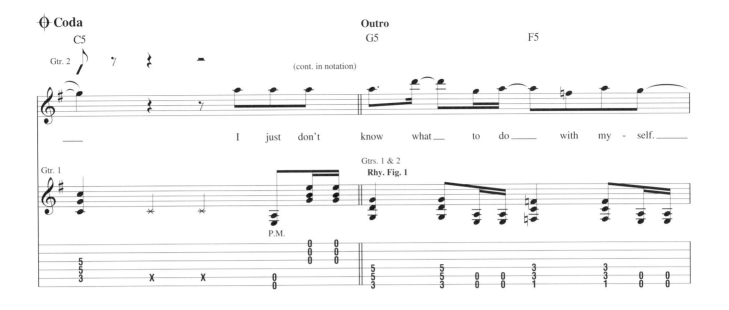

I just don't know what __ to do __ with my - self. __

Just don't know what __ to do __ with my - self. __

Just don't know what __ to do __ with my - self. __ I don't

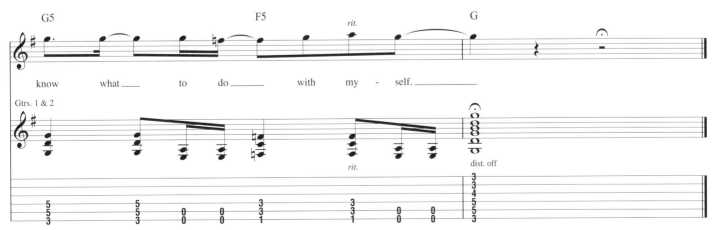

know what __ to do __ with my - self. __

IN THE COLD, COLD NIGHT

Words and Music by
Jack White

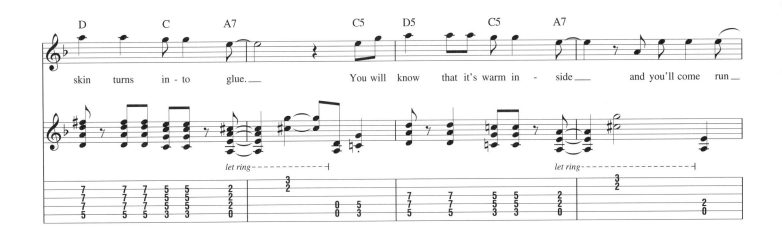

skin turns in-to glue.___ You will know that it's warm in - side___ and you'll come run___

let ring ---------⌐

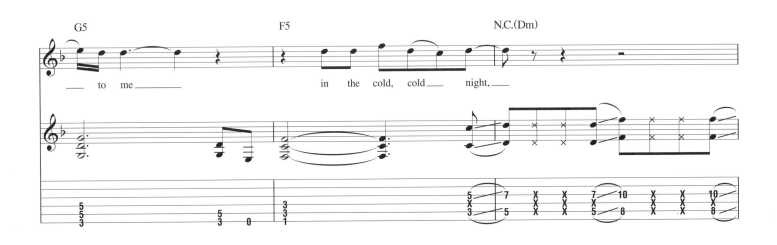

G5   F5   N.C.(Dm)

___ to me _____ in the cold, cold___ night,___

in the cold, cold___ night,___   in the cold, cold   night,___

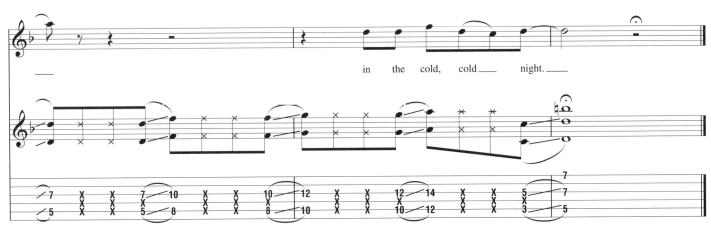

in the cold, cold___ night.___

I WANT TO BE THE BOY TO WARM YOUR MOTHER'S HEART

Words and Music by
Jack White

Gtr. 2: Open G tuning:
(low to high) D-G-D-G-B-D

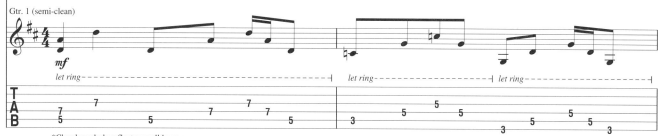

*Chord symbols reflect overall harmony.

while my moth-er baked a lit-tle cake___ for you, and e-ven dread-ed when you said___ good-bye.___

𝄋 **Chorus**

2nd time, Gtr. 2: w/ Fill 1

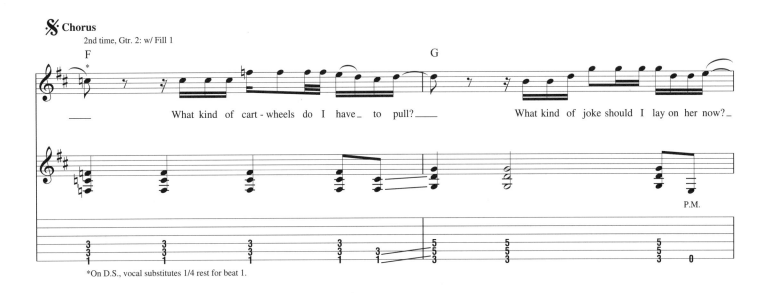

What kind of cart-wheels do I have___ to pull?___ What kind of joke should I lay on her now?___

*On D.S., vocal substitutes 1/4 rest for beat 1.

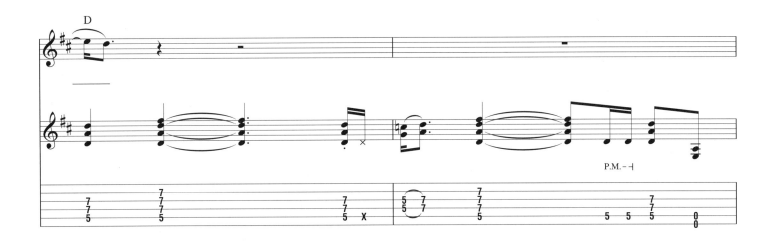

Fill 1
Gtr. 2

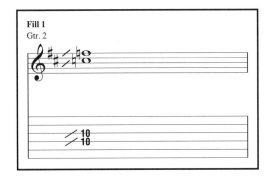

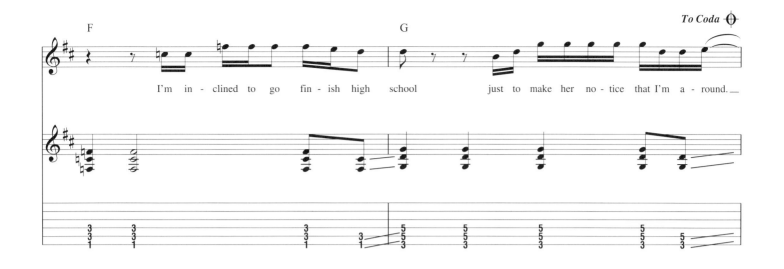

I'm in - clined to go fin - ish high school just to make her no - tice that I'm a - round. __

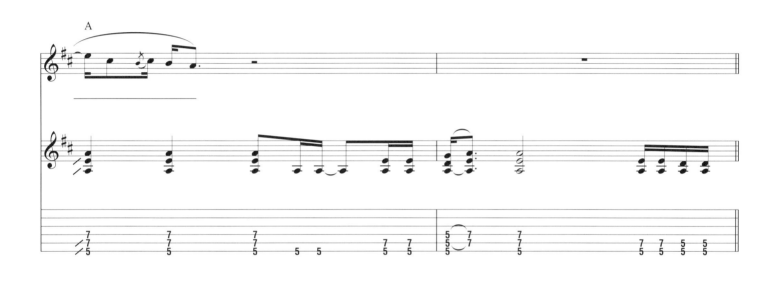

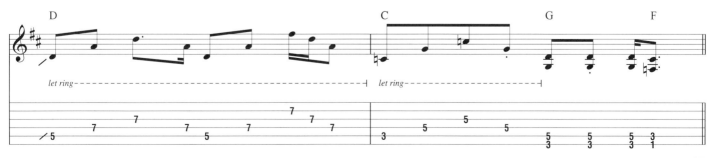

Verse

2. Well, noth-ing I come up with seems_____ to work, feels like ev-'ry-thing I say is a lie._____

And nev-er have I felt like such_____ a jerk, I'm a-fraid to e-ven o-pen my eyes._____

Be-cause I real-ly don't want her to judge_____ me, I want her to real-ly know who I am._____

And then, and on-ly then will she love_____ me, well, at least that was_____ the plan._____

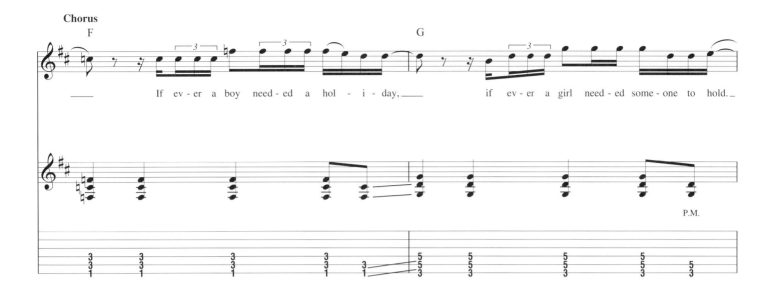

If ev-er a boy need-ed a hol - i - day, ___ if ev-er a girl need-ed some-one to hold. __

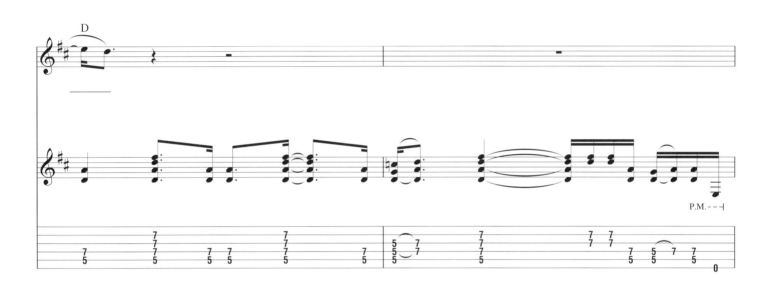

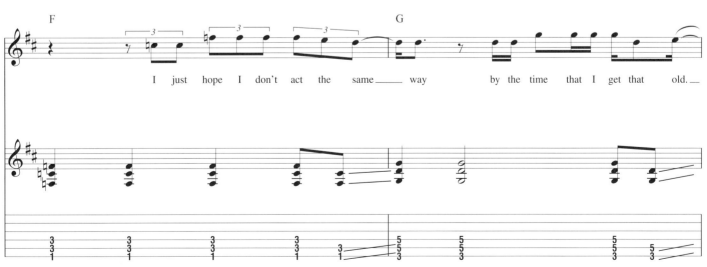

I just hope I don't act the same ___ way by the time that I get that old. __

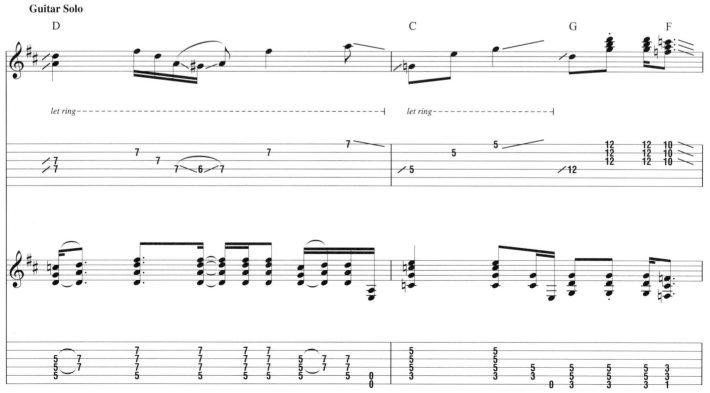

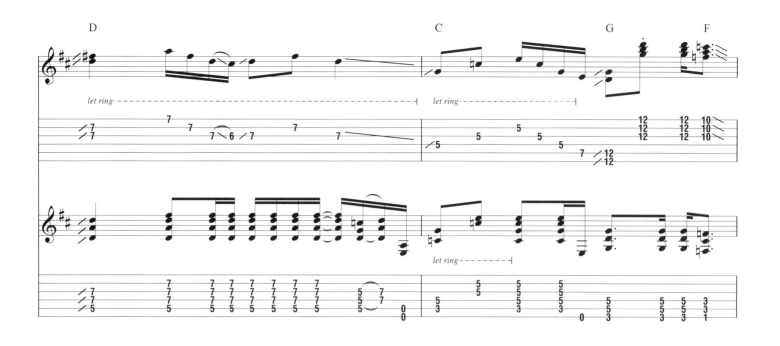

D.S. al Coda

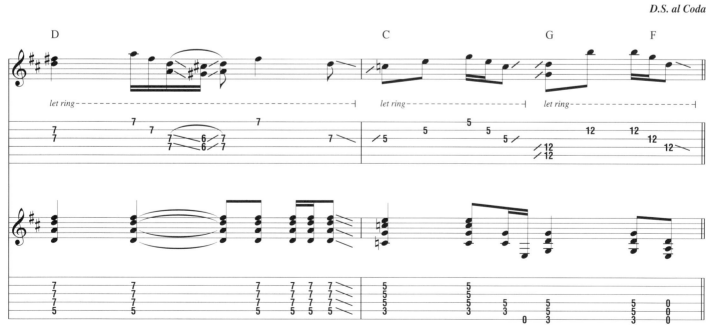

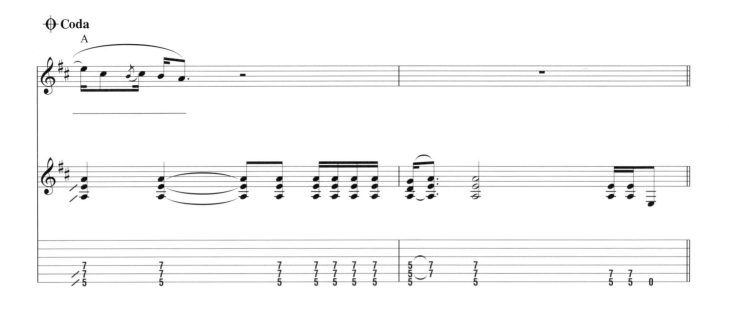

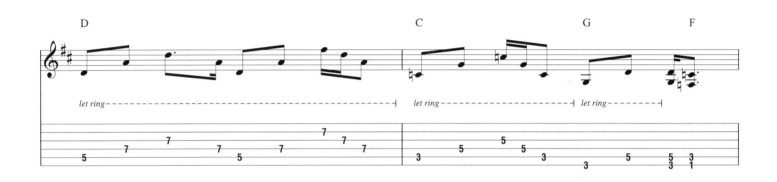

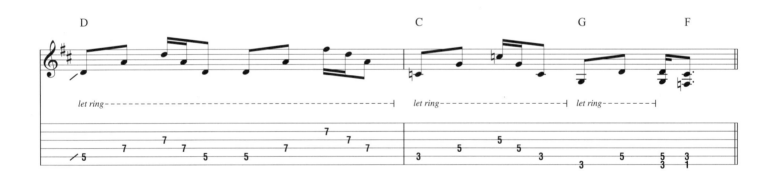

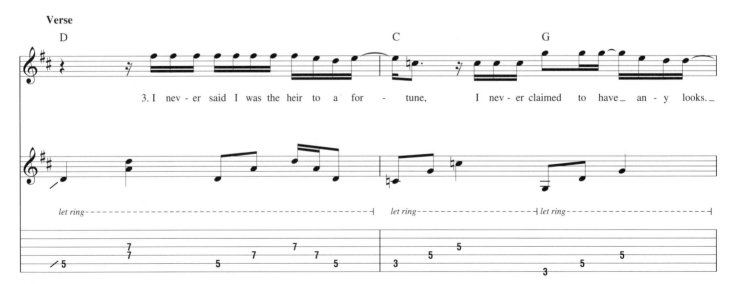

3. I nev - er said I was the heir to a for - tune, I nev - er claimed to have_ an - y looks._

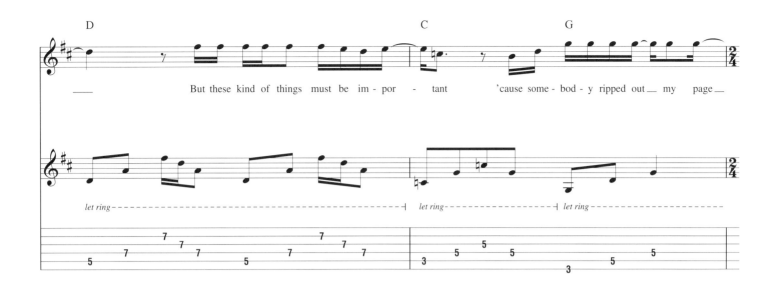

But these kind of things must be im-por- -tant 'cause some-bod- y ripped out_ my page_

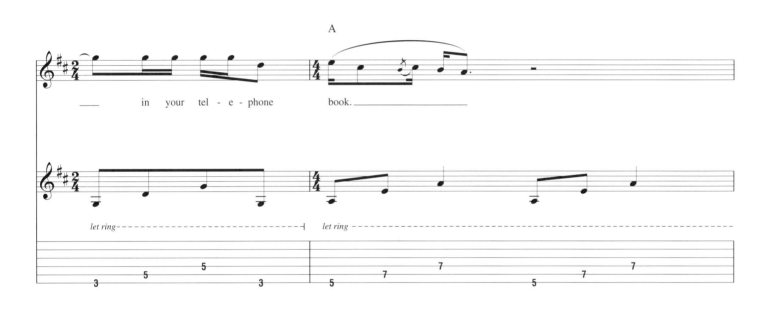

in your tel - e - phone book._

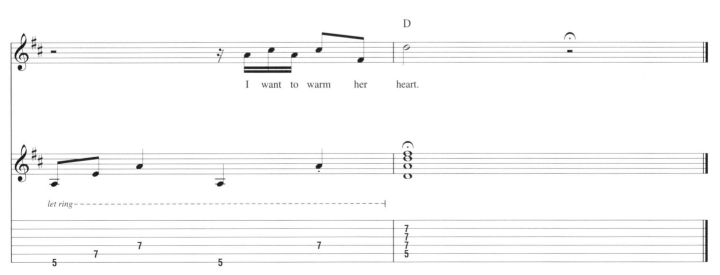

I want to warm her heart.

YOU'VE GOT HER IN YOUR POCKET

Words and Music by
Jack White

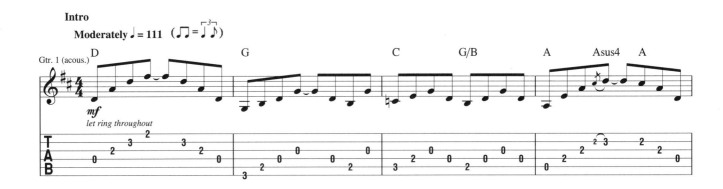

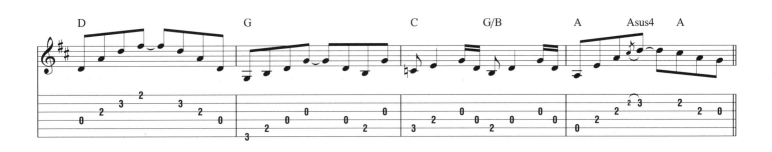

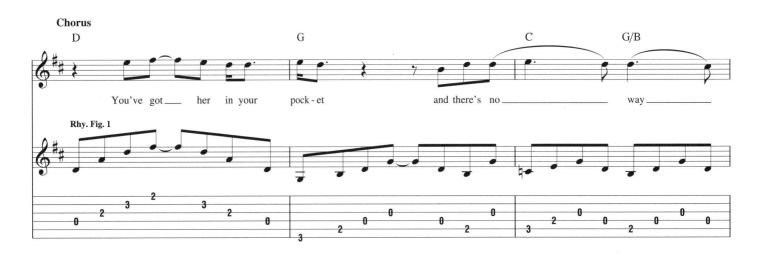

You've got ___ her in your pock-et and there's no ___ way ___

out now. Put it in the safe and lock it 'cause it's home ___

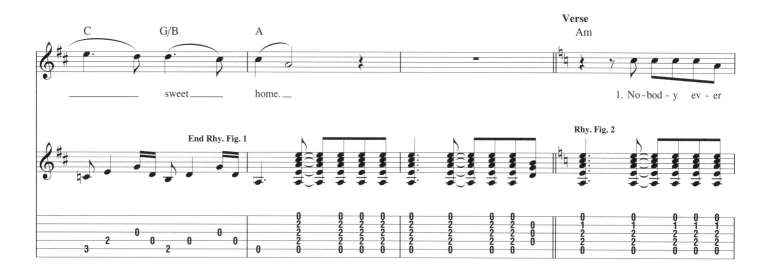

sweet _____ home. _____

1. No - bod - y ev - er

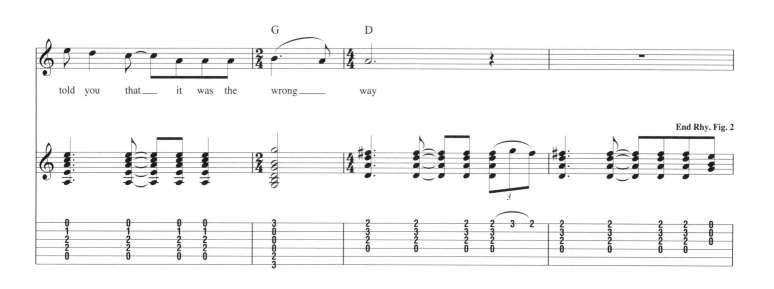

told you that ___ it was the wrong _____ way

Gtr. 1: w/ Rhy. Fig. 2

to trick a wom - an, make her feel ___ she did it her _____ way. _____

And you'll be there _____ if she ev - er feels

BALL AND BISCUIT

Words and Music by
Jack White

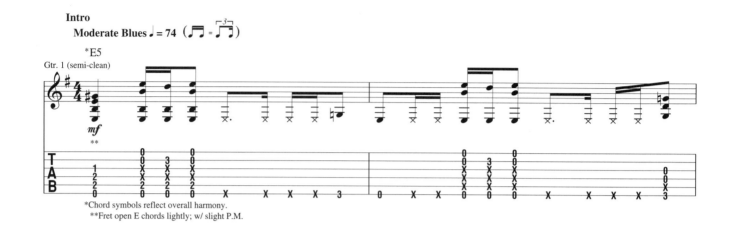

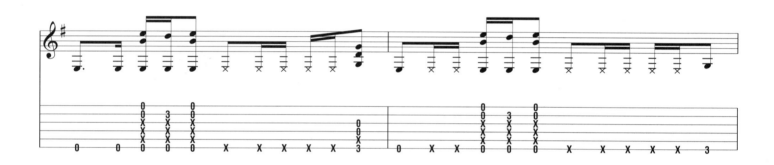

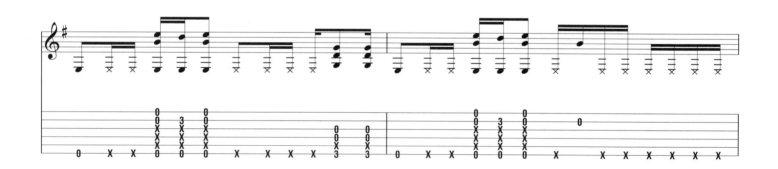

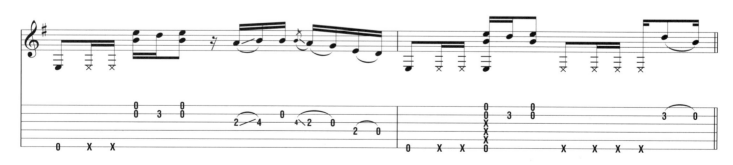

*Chord symbols reflect overall harmony.
**Fret open E chords lightly; w/ slight P.M.

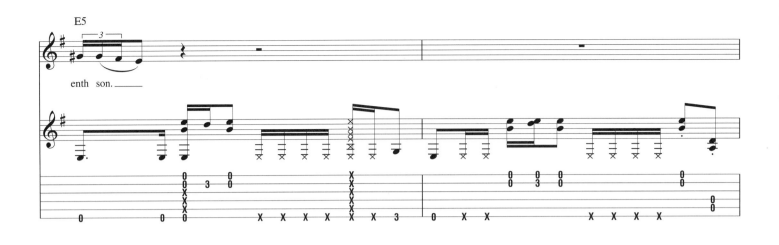

enth son. ____

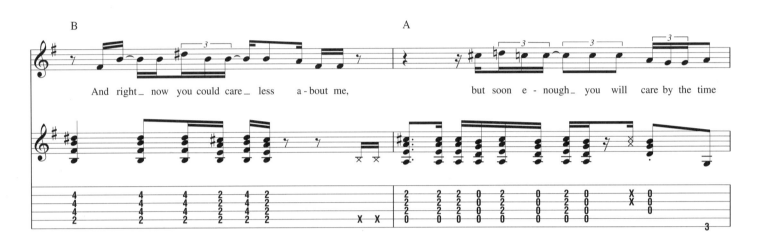

And right ____ now you could care ____ less ____ a - bout me, ____ but soon e - nough ____ you will care by the time

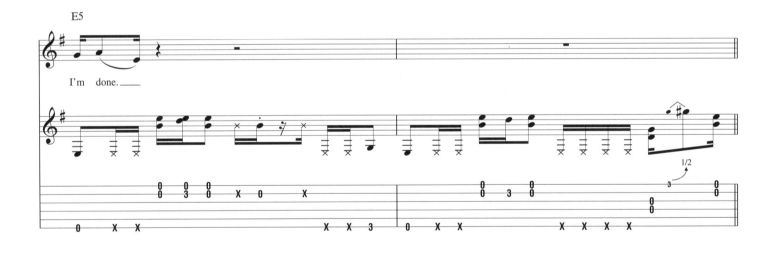

I'm done. ____

Chorus

N.C.(E5)

Let's have a ball and a bis - quit, sug - ar, ____ and ____ take our sweet lit - tle time ____

let ring

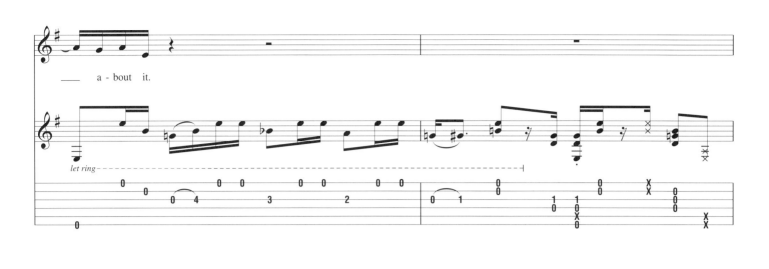

_ a - bout it.

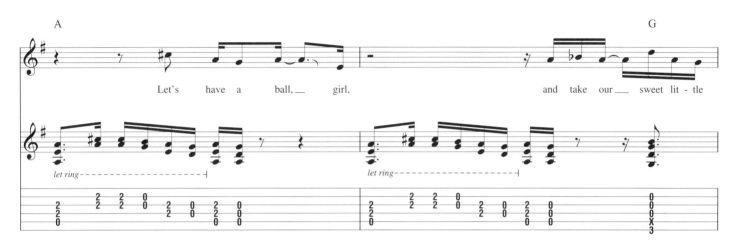

Let's have a ball, _ girl, and take our _ sweet lit - tle

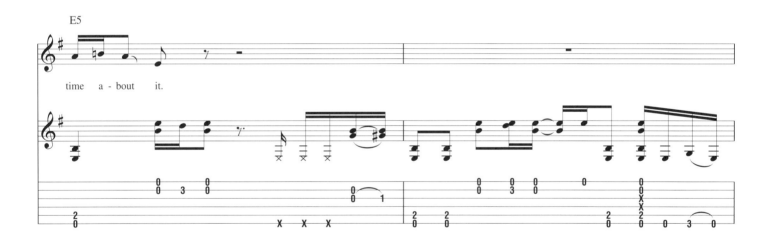

time a - bout it.

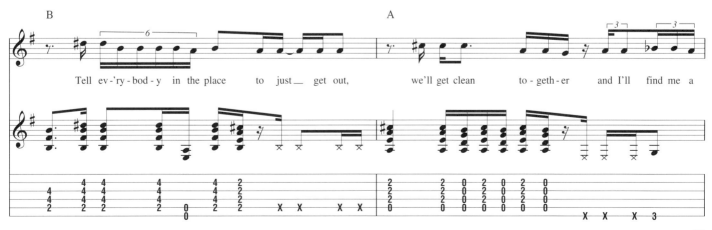

Tell ev-'ry-bod-y in the place to just _ get out, we'll get clean to-geth-er and I'll find me a

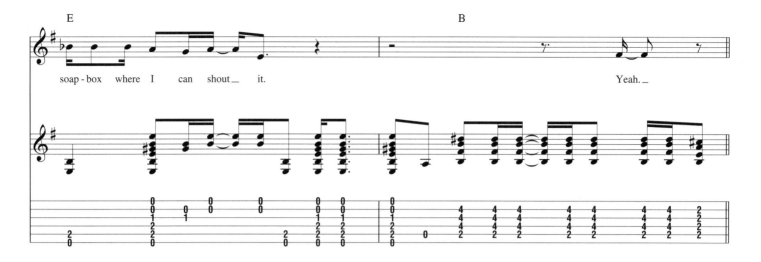

soap-box where I can shout _ it.

Yeah. _

Guitar Solo

E5

Gtr. 2 (dist.)

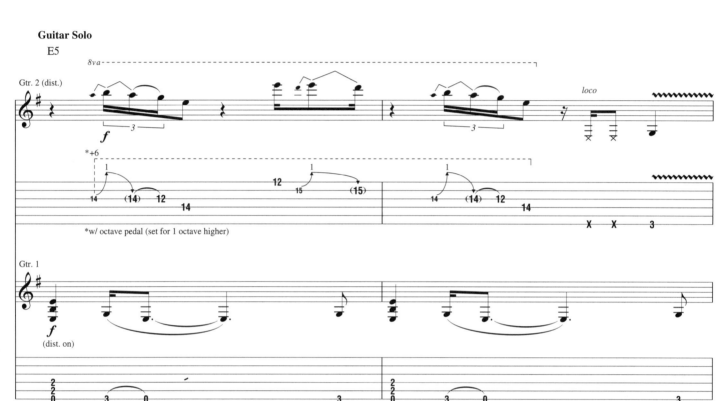

*w/ octave pedal (set for 1 octave higher)

Gtr. 1

(dist. on)

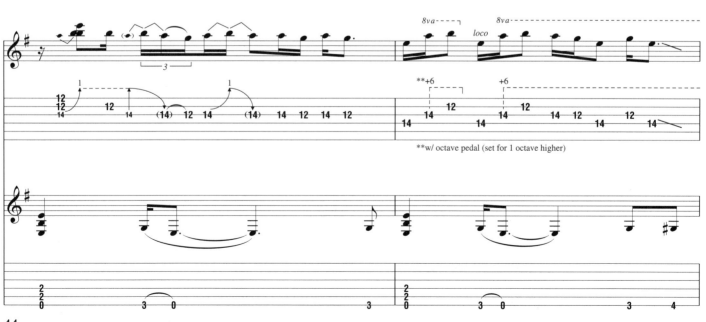

**w/ octave pedal (set for 1 octave higher)

44

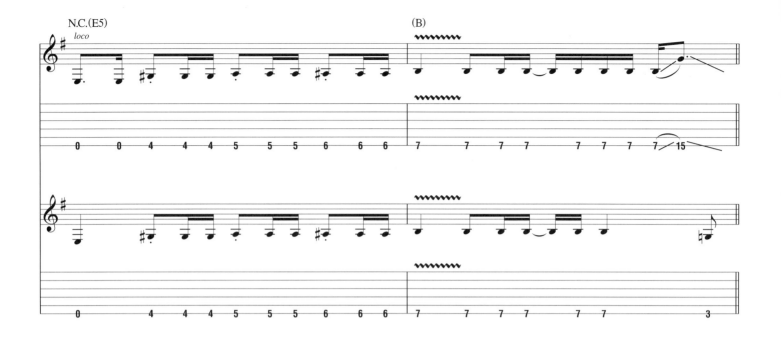

Interlude

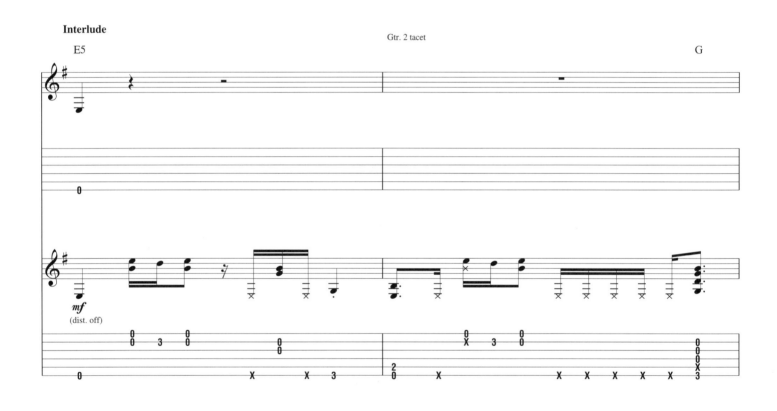

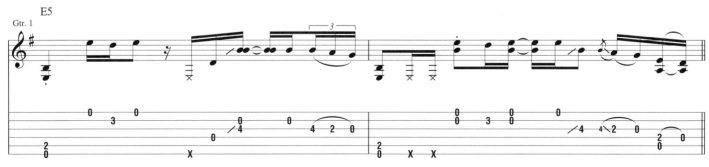

that my strength is ten fold, girl. I'll let you see it if you want to be-fore you go.

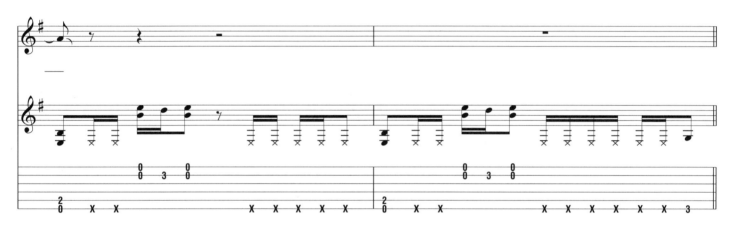

Chorus

N.C.(E5)

Let's have a ball and a bis - quit, sug - ar, and take our sweet lit - tle time

let ring

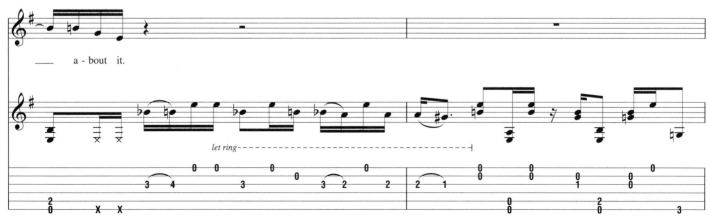

a - bout it.

let ring

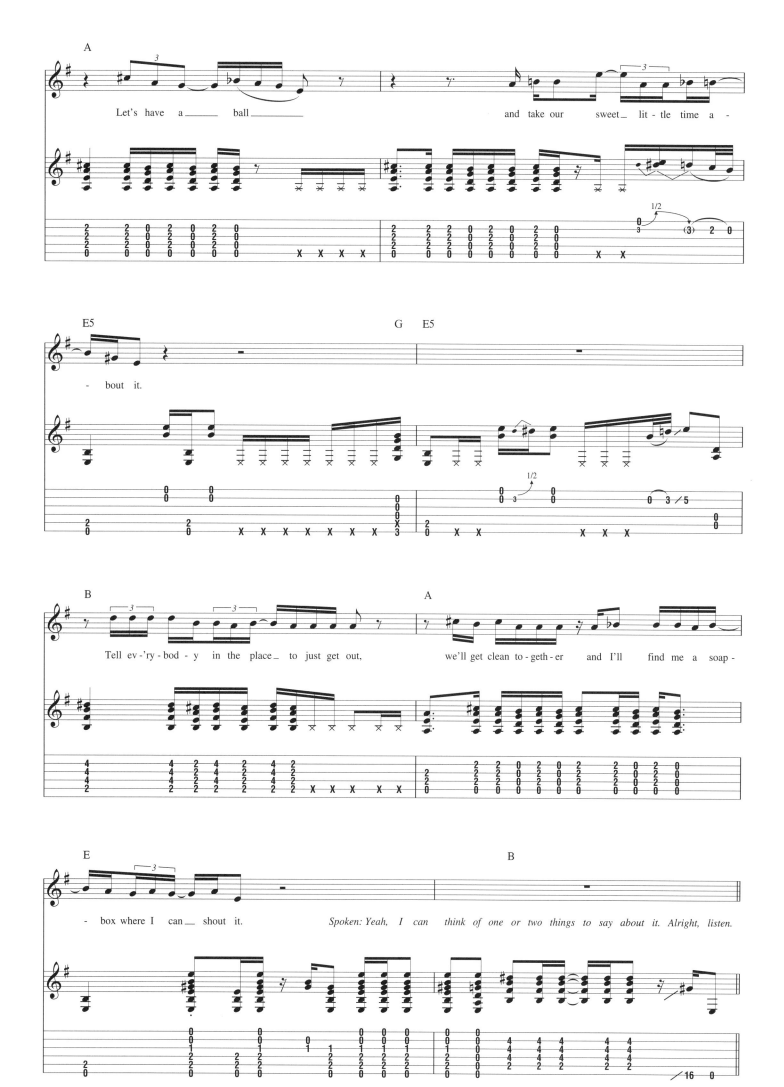

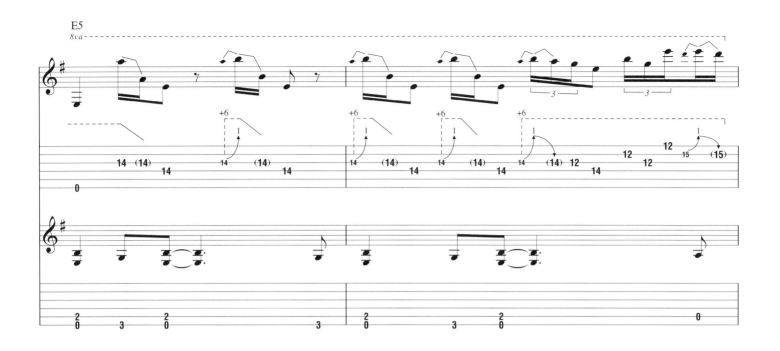

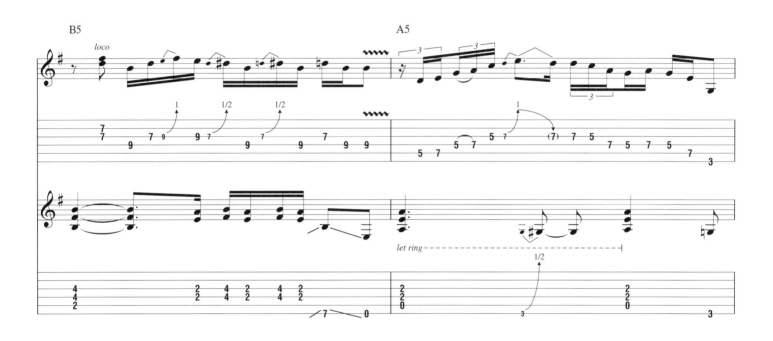

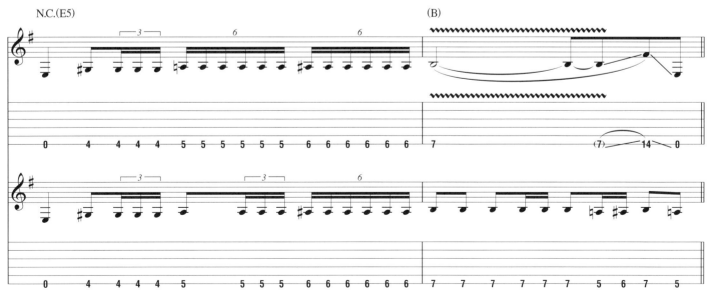

51

Interlude

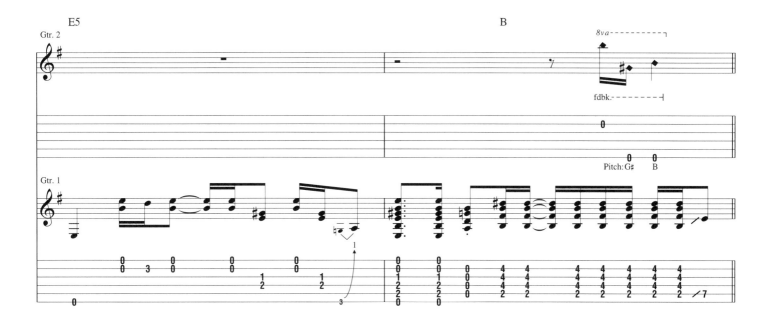

Guitar Solo

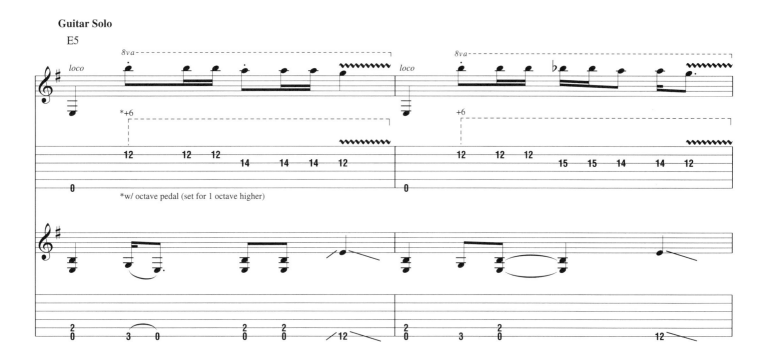

*w/ octave pedal (set for 1 octave higher)

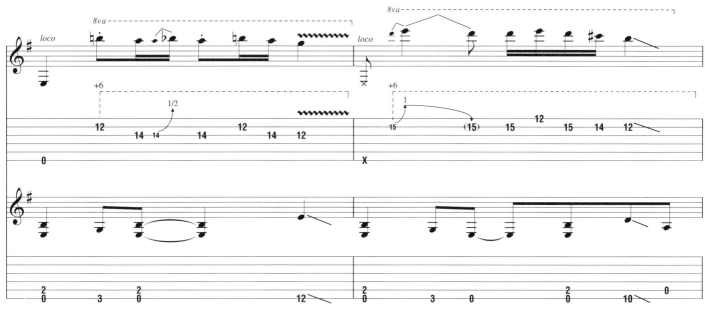

A5

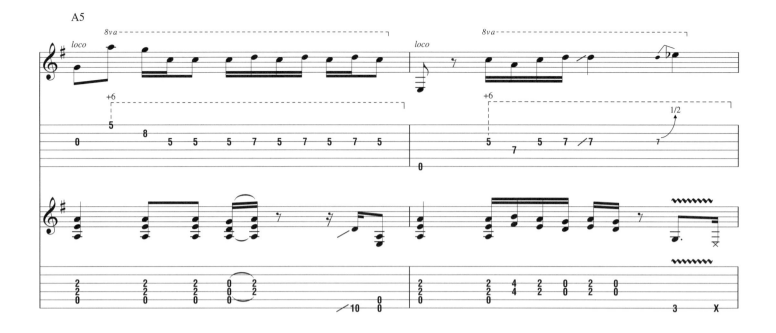

E5

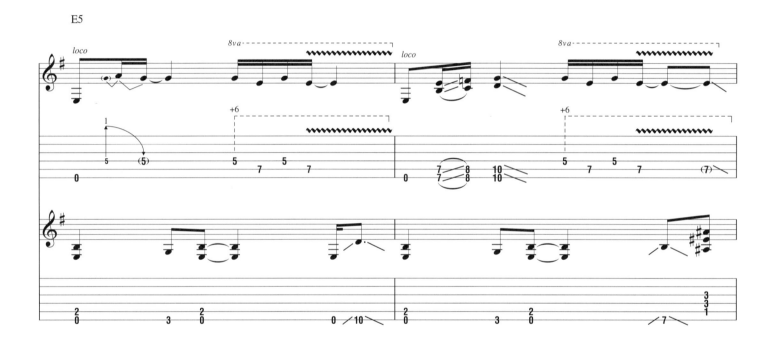

B5   **A5**

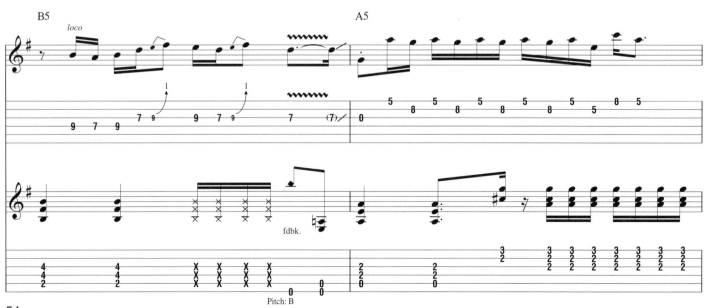

54

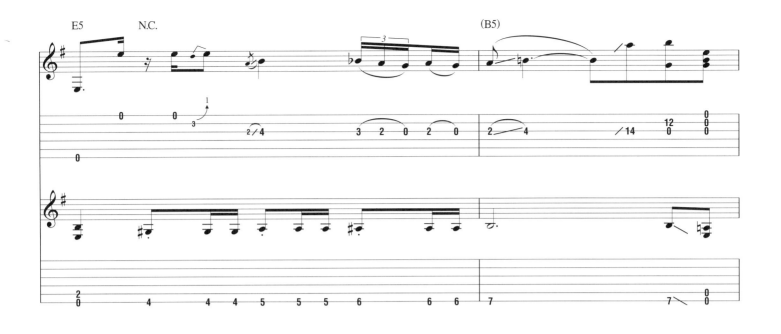

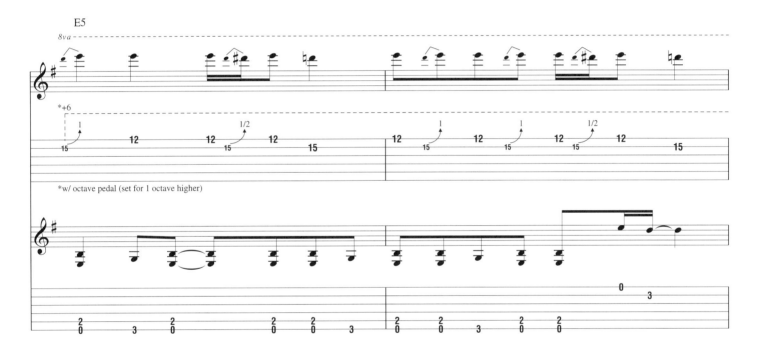

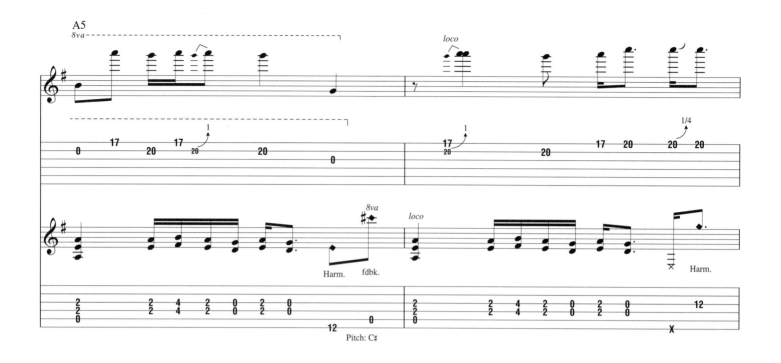

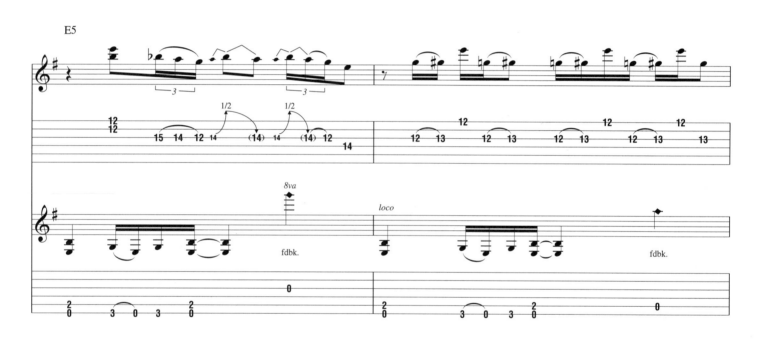

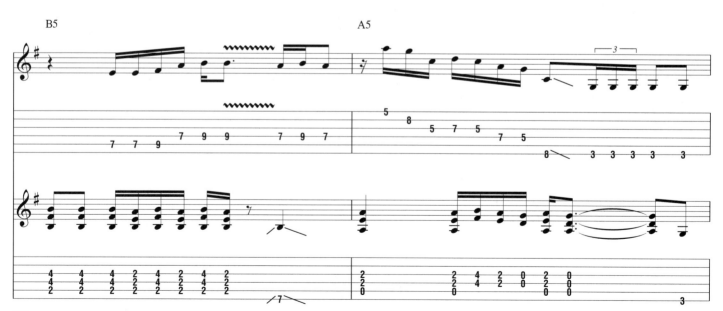

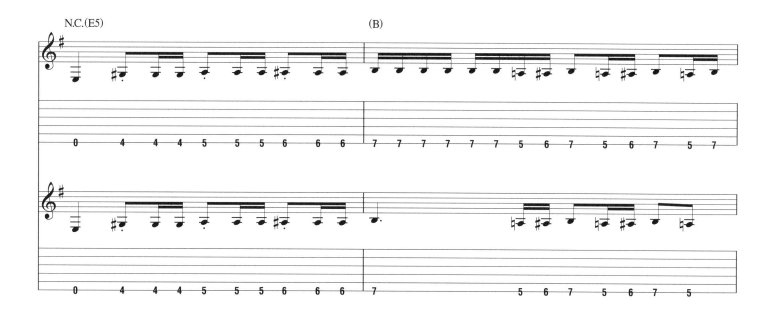

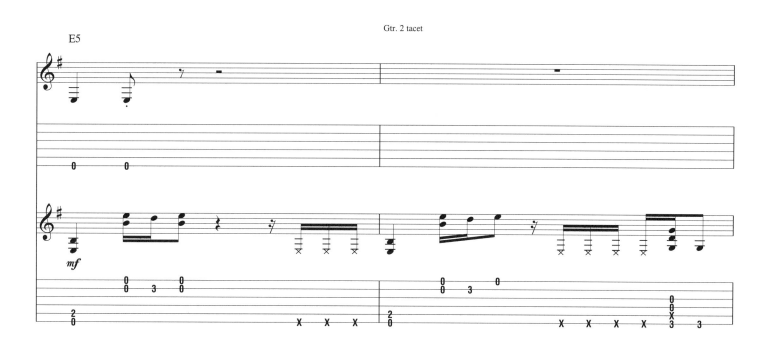

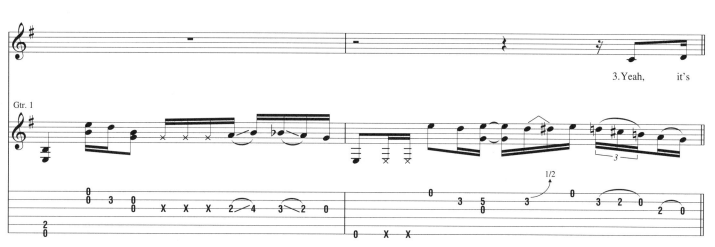

Verse

N.C.(E5)

quite pos - si - ble that I'm your third man, but it's a fact that I'm the sev - enth son.

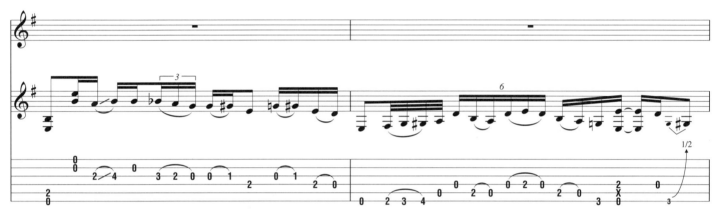

(A5)

It was the oth - er two which made me your third, but it's my ___ moth - er who made me the sev - enth ___

(E5)   G5

___ son.

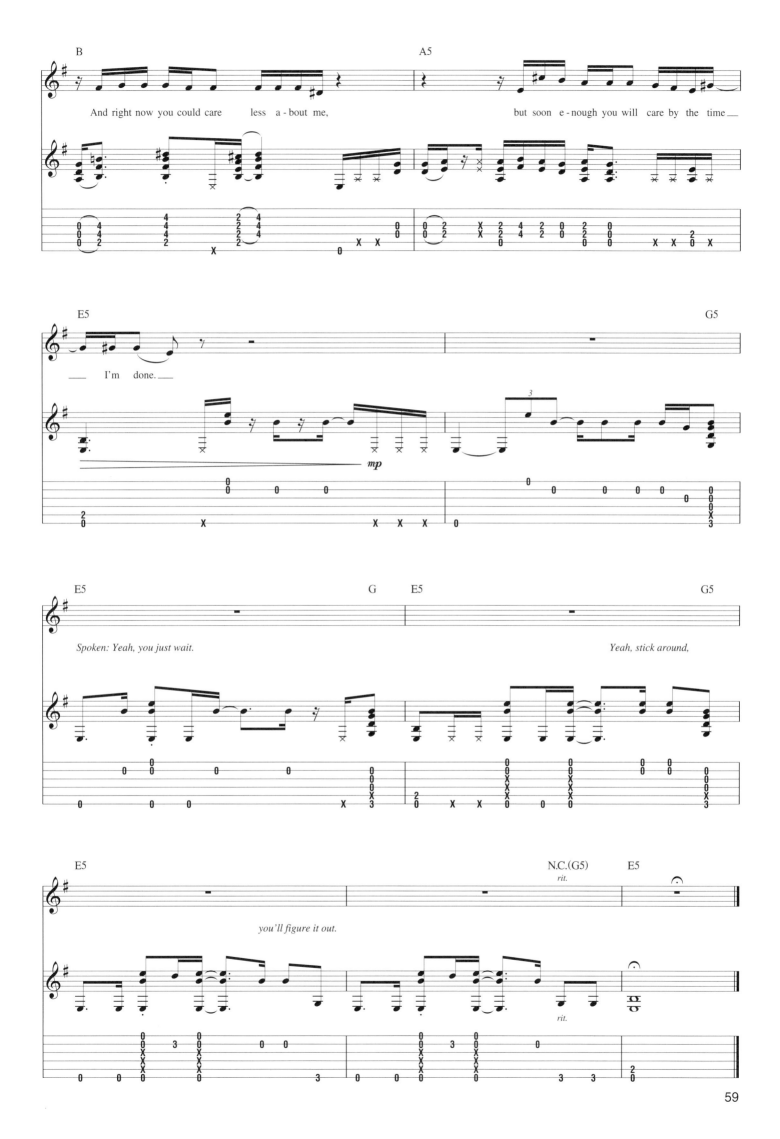

THE HARDEST BUTTON TO BUTTON

Words and Music by
Jack White

Intro
Moderate Rock ♩ = 128

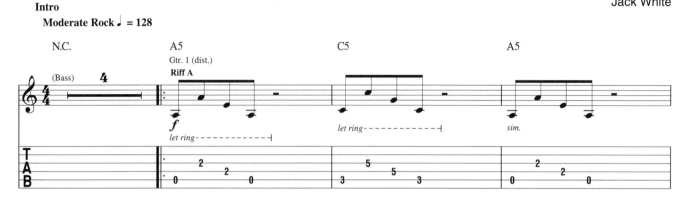

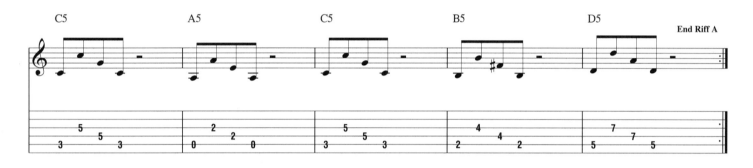

Verse
Gtr. 1: w/ Riff A

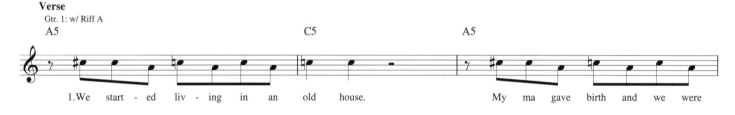

1.We start-ed liv-ing in an old house. My ma gave birth and we were

check-ing it out.___ It was a ba-by boy so we bought him a toy, it was a

ray gun, and it was nine-teen eight-y one. We named him "Ba-by." He had a

tooth-ache. He start-ed cry-ing, it sound-ed like an earth-quake. It did-n't

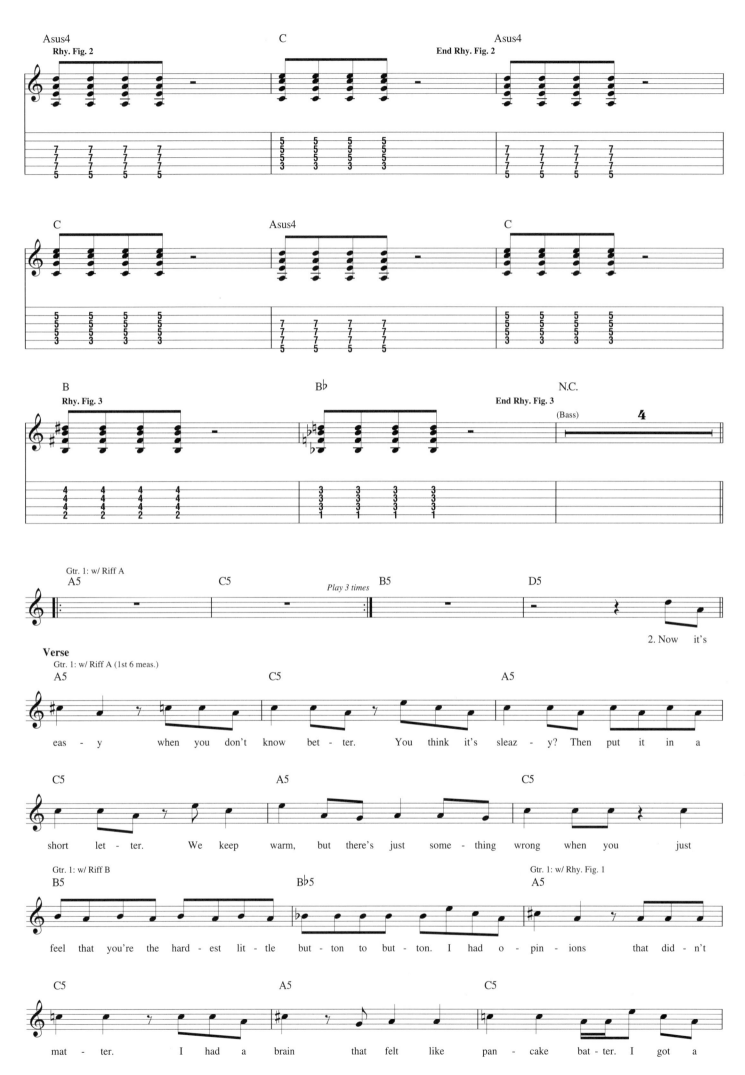

2. Now it's

Verse

eas - y when you don't know bet - ter. You think it's sleaz - y? Then put it in a

short let - ter. We keep warm, but there's just some - thing wrong when you just

feel that you're the hard - est lit - tle but - ton to but - ton. I had o - pin - ions that did - n't

mat - ter. I had a brain that felt like pan - cake bat - ter. I got a

LITTLE ACORNS

Words and Music by
Jack White

Intro

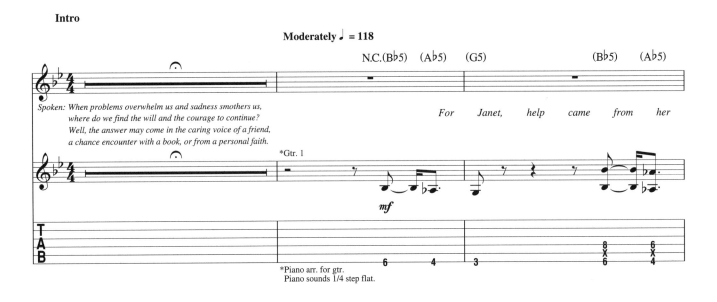

*Piano arr. for gtr.
Piano sounds 1/4 step flat.

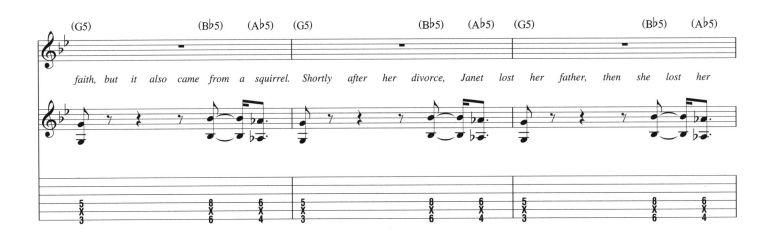

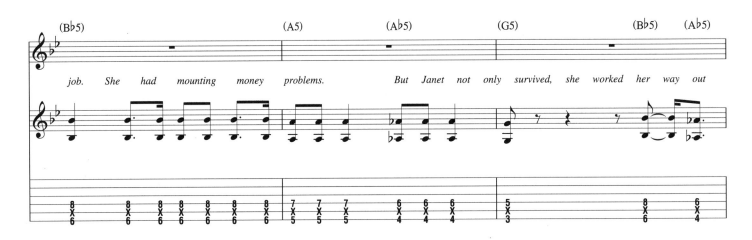

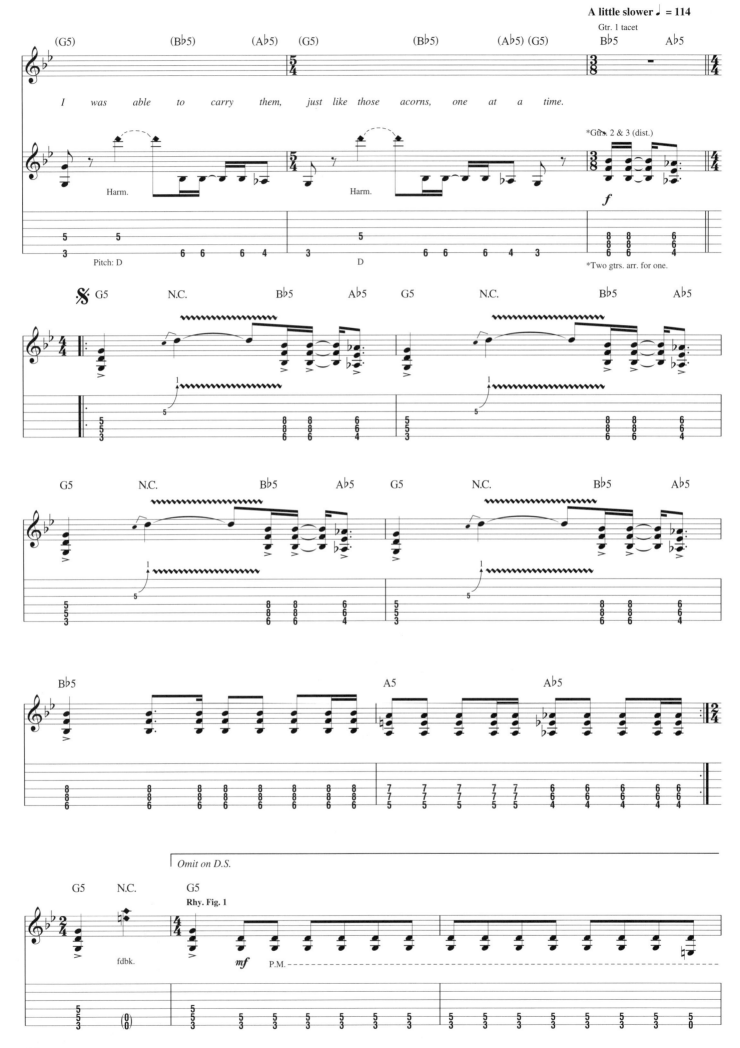

I was able to carry them, just like those acorns, one at a time.

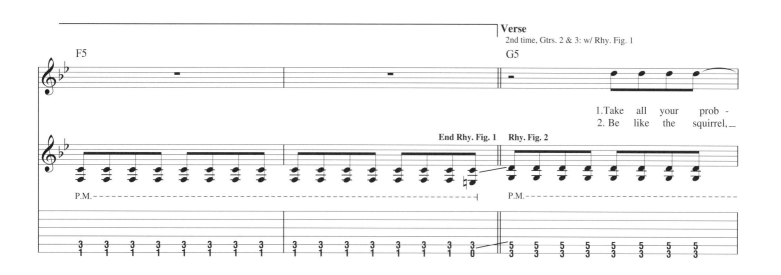

1.Take all your prob -
2. Be like the squirrel,

- lems and rip 'em a - part, _____ oh, _____ oh, _____ oh, oh, oh. _____
_____ girl, be like the squirrel, _____ oh, _____ oh, _____ oh, oh, oh. _____

Gtrs. 2 & 3: w/ Rhy. Fig. 2 (2 1/2 times)

Car - ry them off _____ in a shop - ping cart, _____ oh,
Give it a whirl, _____ girl, be like the squirrel, _____ oh,

_____ oh, _____ oh, oh, oh. _____ An - oth - er thing you _____ should -'ve known _____ from the start, _____
_____ oh, _____ oh, oh, oh. And an - oth - er thing you _____ have to know _____ in this world, _____

_____ oh, _____ oh, oh, oh, oh, oh. _____ The prob - lems at hand _____
_____ oh, _____ oh, oh, oh, oh. _____ Cut up your hair,

67

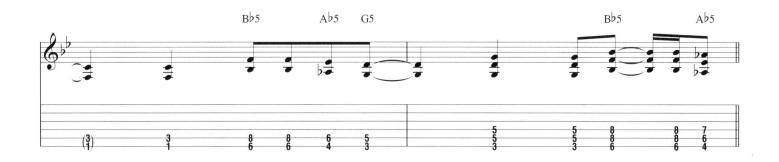

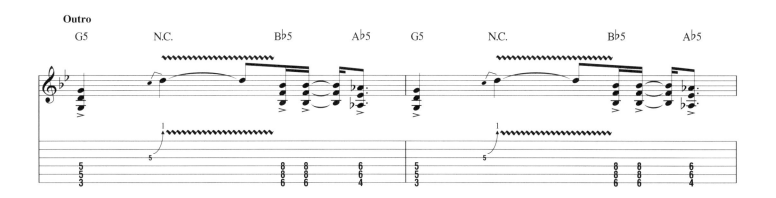

Outro

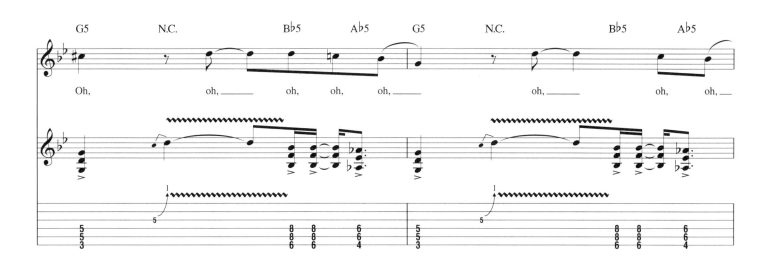

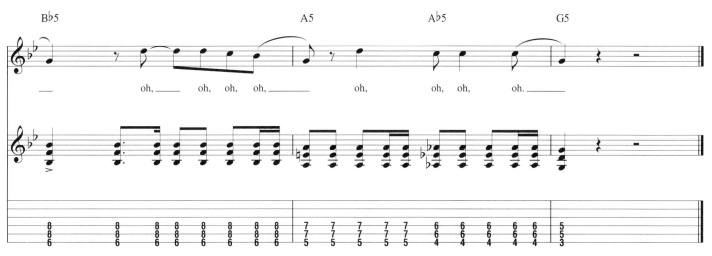

HYPNOTIZE

Words and Music by
Jack White

Intro
Fast Rock ♩ = 184

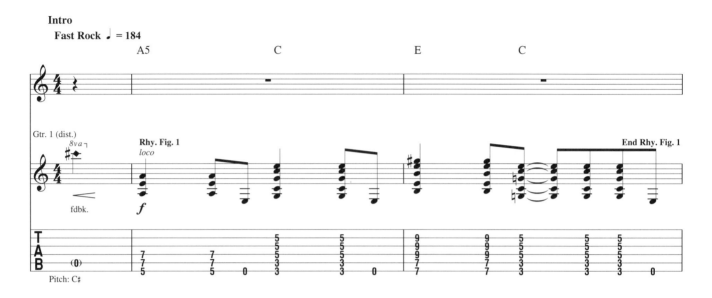

Verse

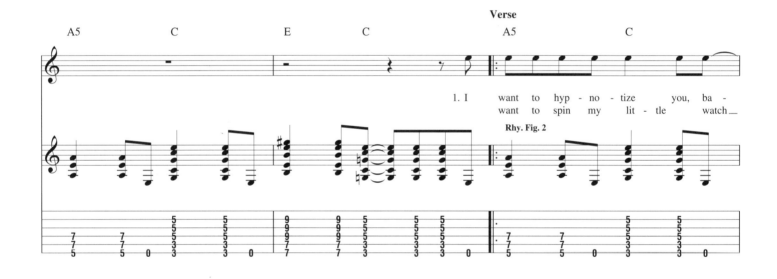

1. I want to hyp - no - tize you, ba -
   want to spin my lit - tle watch

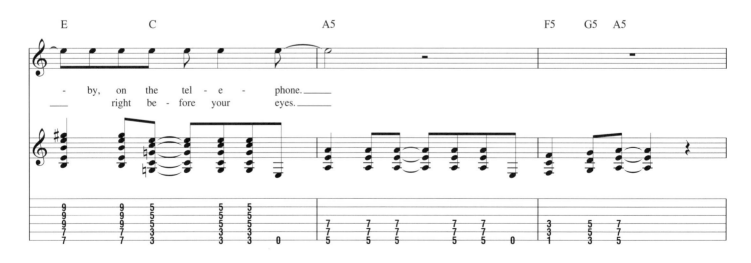

- by, on the tel - e - phone._____
right be - fore your eyes._____

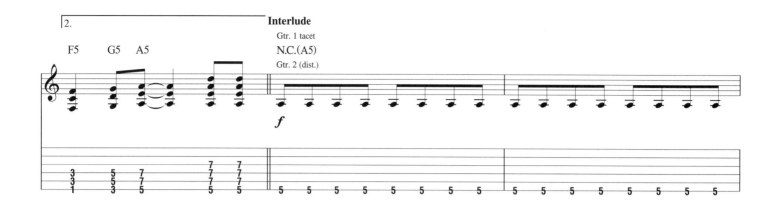

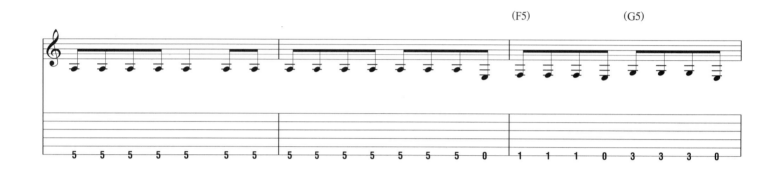

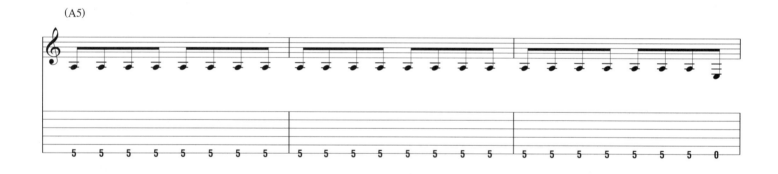

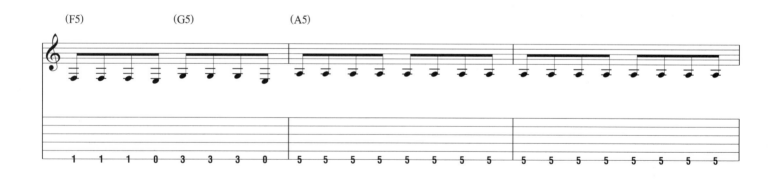

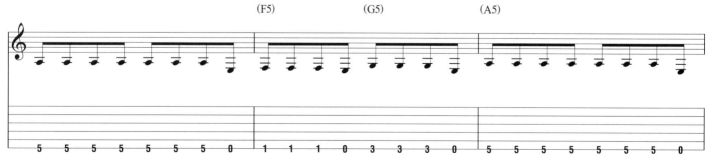

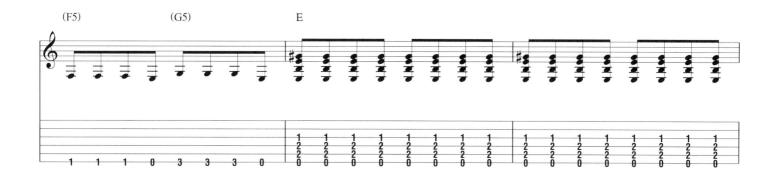

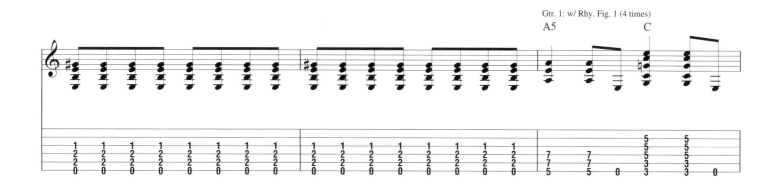

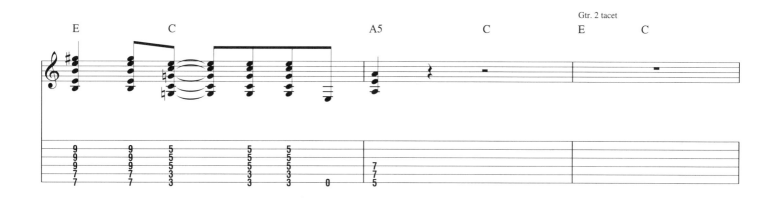

3. I

Verse

Gtr. 1: w/ Rhy. Fig. 2

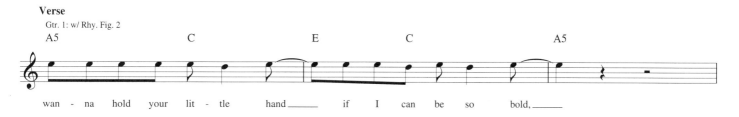

wan - na hold your lit - tle hand_____ if I can be so bold,_____

and be your right hand man till your hand gets old.

And then when all the feel-ing's gone, _____ just de-

cide if you want to keep hold-ing on. I want to hold your lit-tle hand _____

_____ if I can be so bold, _____ if I can be so bold, _____

if I can be so bold. _____

THE AIR NEAR MY FINGERS

Words and Music by
Jack White

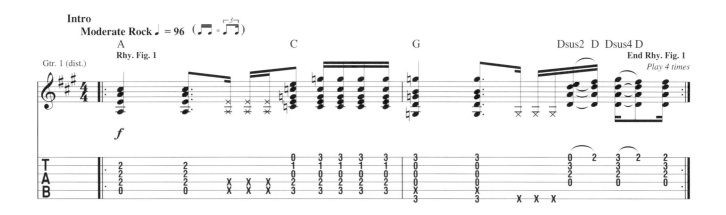

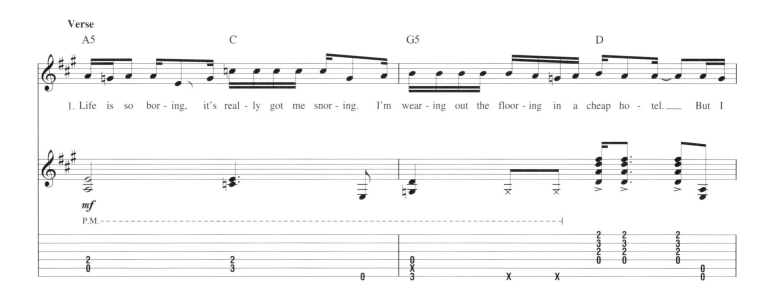

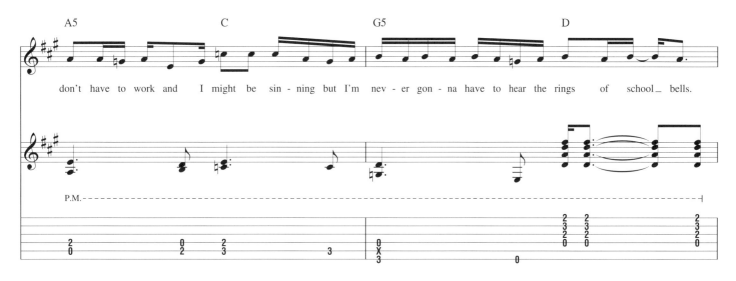

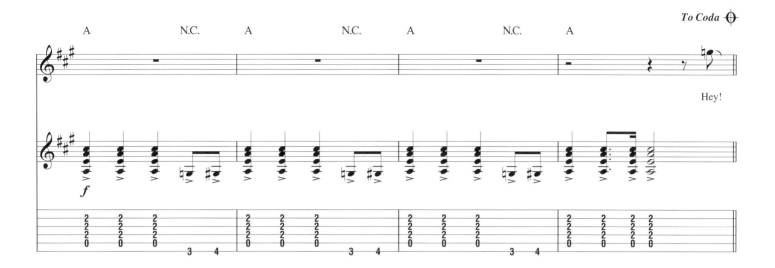

Hey!

Interlude

Gtr. 1: w/ Rhy. Fig. 1 (2 times)

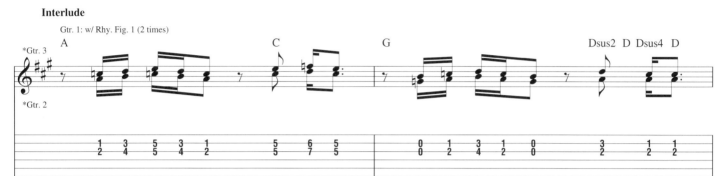

*Keyboards arr. for gtr.

D.S. al Coda

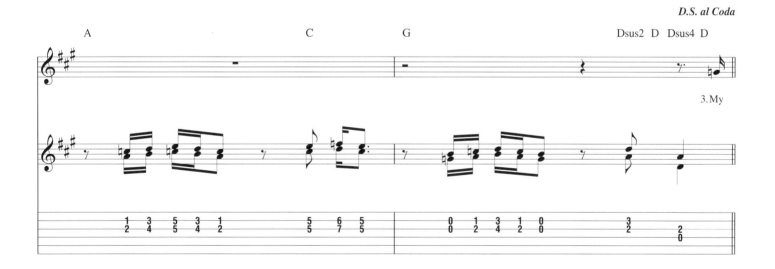

3. My

⊕**Coda**

Outro

Gtr. 1: w/ Rhy. Fig. 1

Fade out

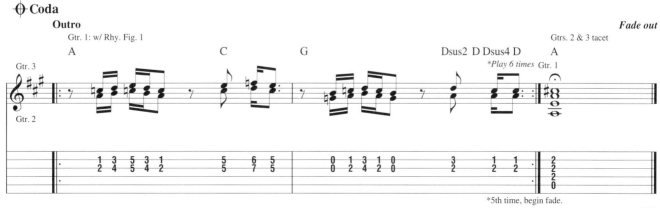

*5th time, begin fade.

GIRL, YOU HAVE NO FAITH IN MEDICINE

Words and Music by
Jack White

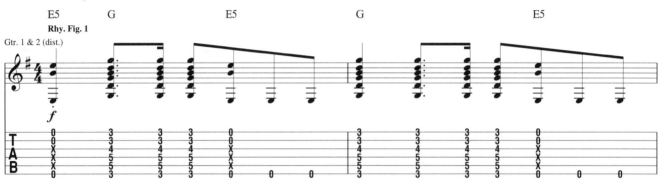

Intro

Moderately fast Rock ♩ = 152

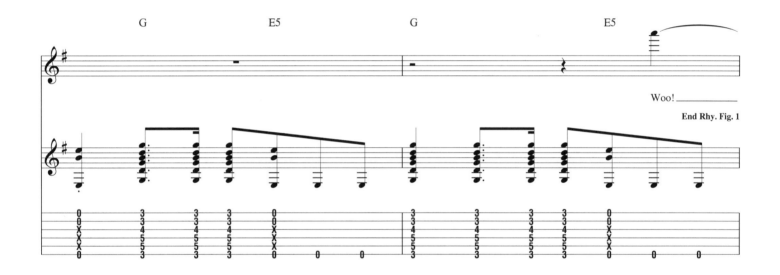

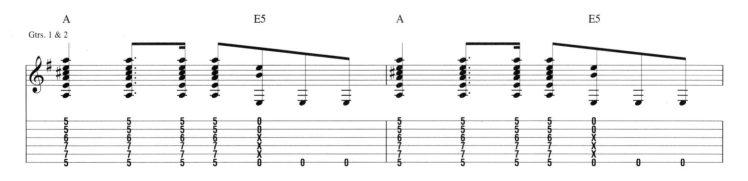

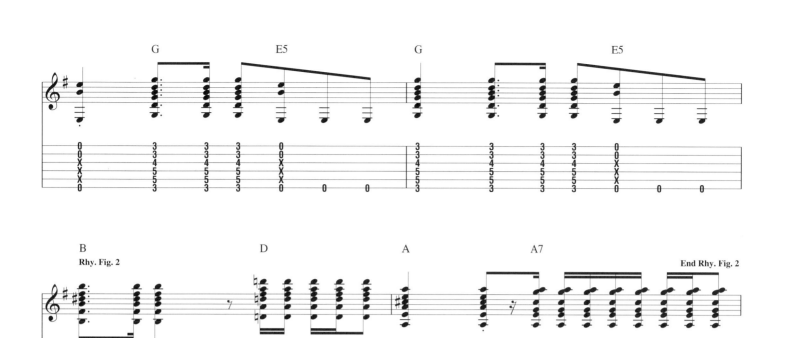

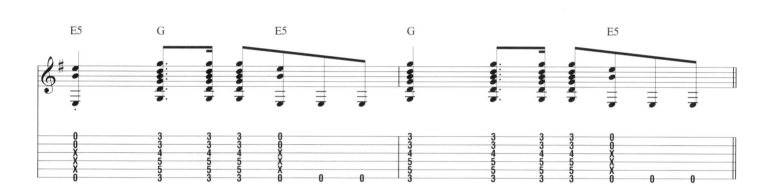

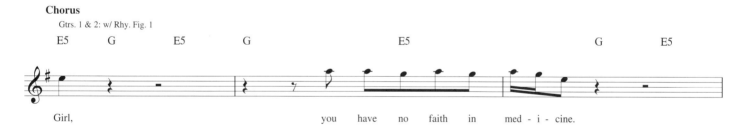

Chorus

Gtrs. 1 & 2: w/ Rhy. Fig. 1

Girl,   you have no faith in med - i - cine.

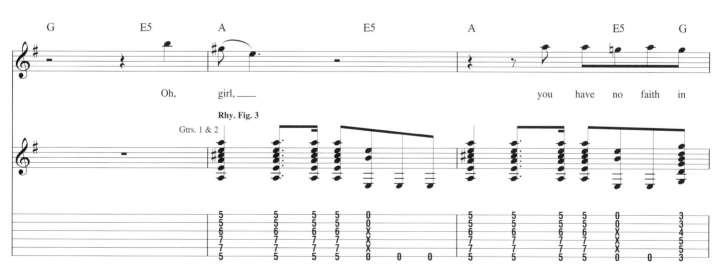

Oh,   girl, ___   you have no faith in

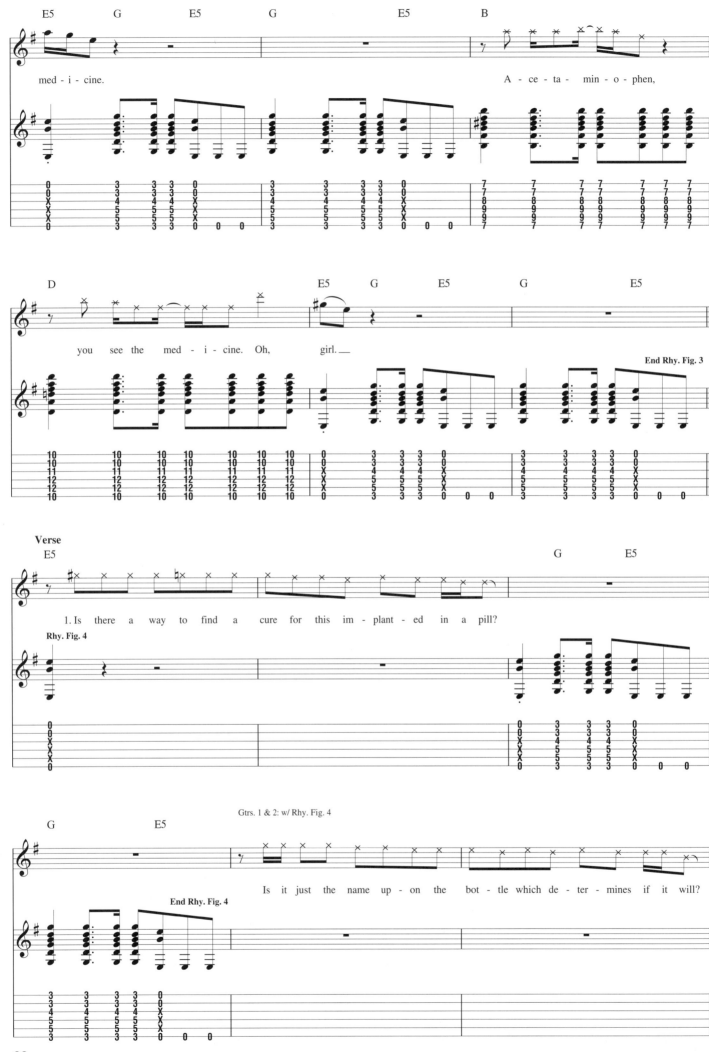

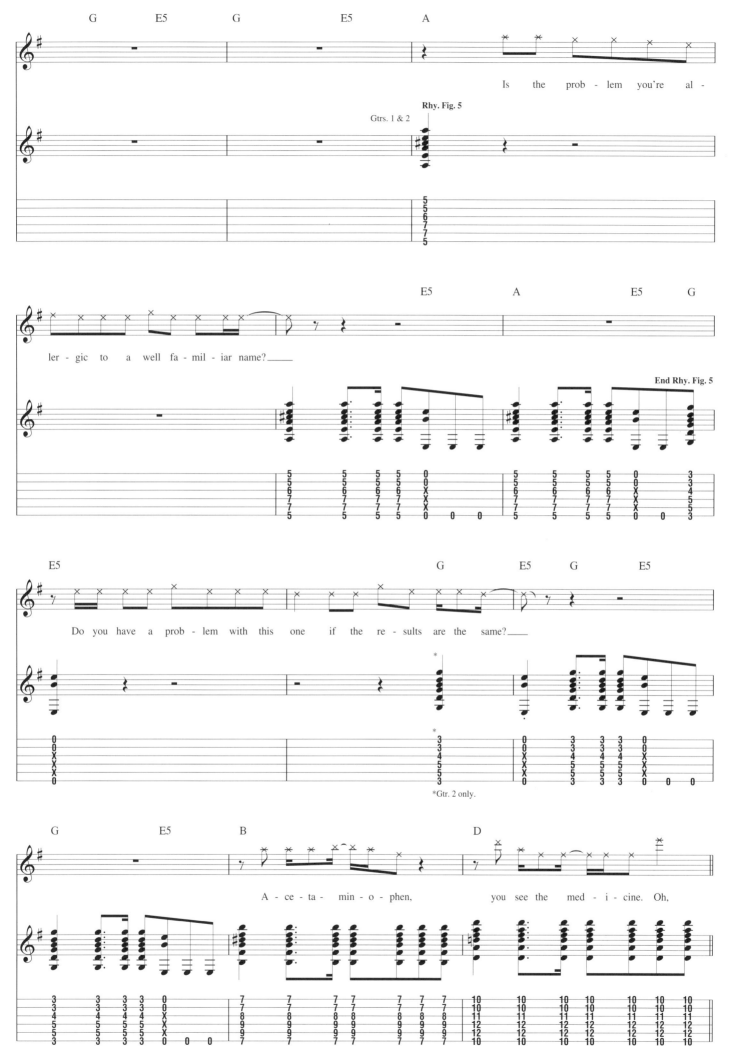

Chorus

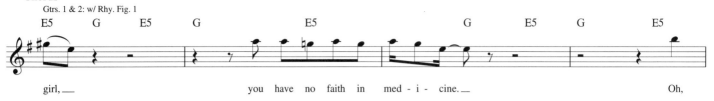

girl, ___ you have no faith in med - i - cine. ___ Oh,

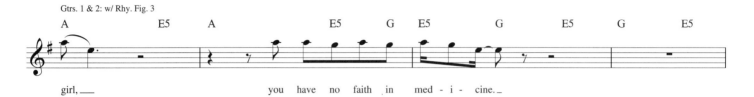

girl, ___ you have no faith in med - i - cine. ___

A - ce - ta - min - o - phen, you see the med - i - cine. Oh, girl. ___

Guitar Solo

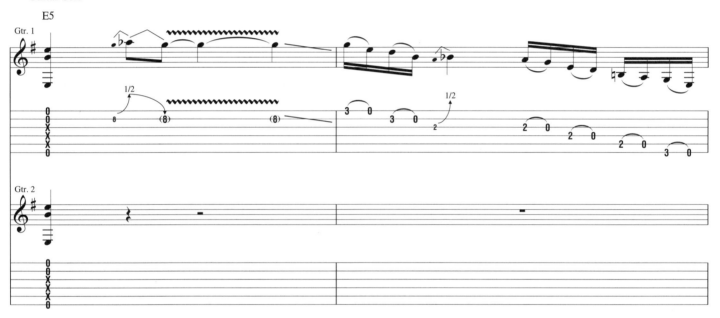

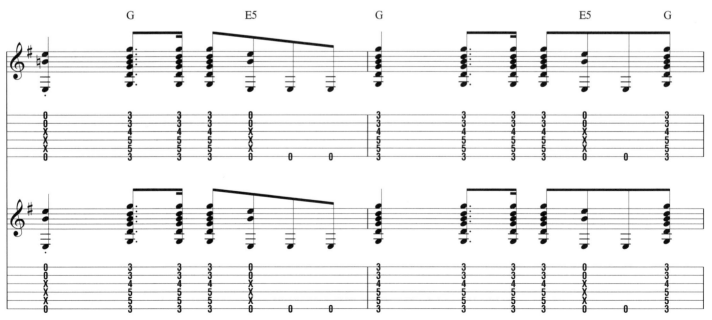

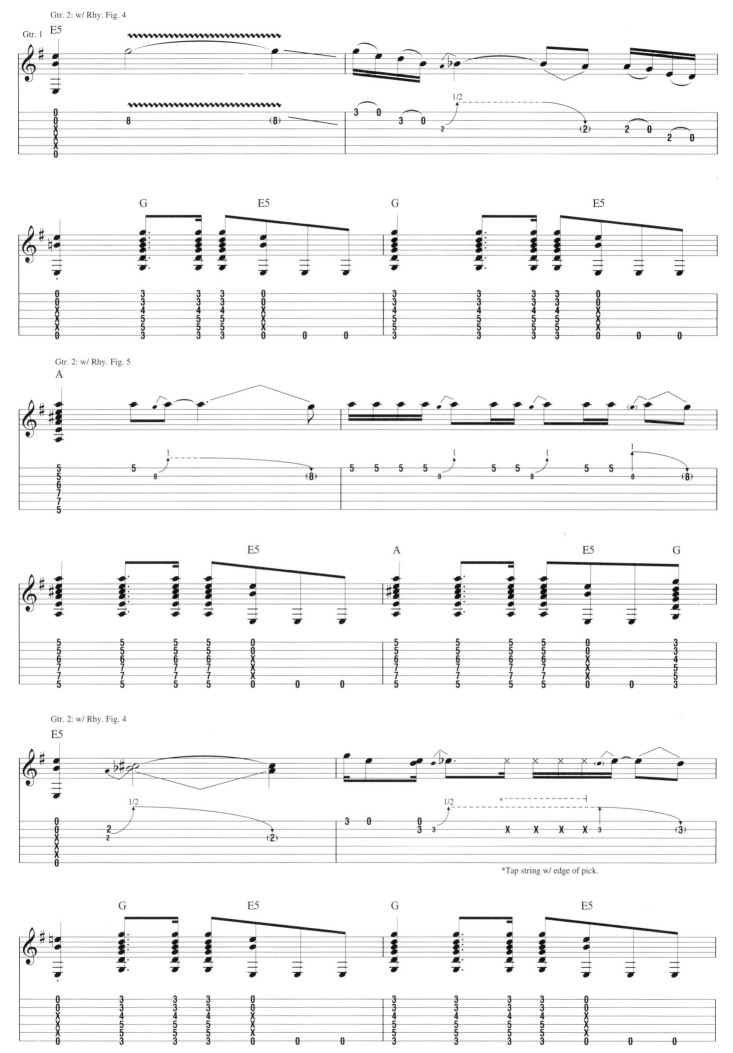

*Tap string w/ edge of pick.

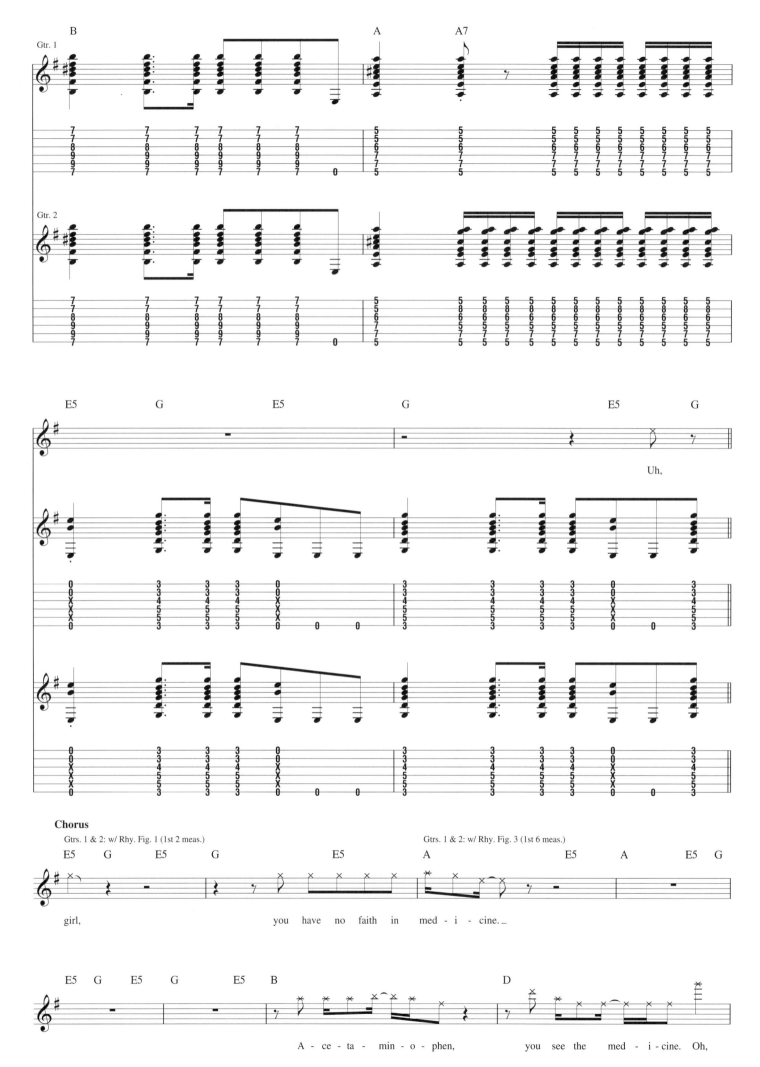

Chorus

Gtrs. 1 & 2: w/ Rhy. Fig. 1 (1st 2 meas.)   Gtrs. 1 & 2: w/ Rhy. Fig. 3 (1st 6 meas.)

girl,   you have no faith in med - i - cine. _

A - ce - ta - min - o - phen,   you see the med - i - cine. Oh,

girl. ____

Gtrs. 1 & 2

Verse

2. Well, strip the bark right off the tree and just hand it this way.

*Rake strings behind the nut.

Don't e - ven need a drink of

wa - ter to make the head - ache go a - way.

*As before

WELL IT'S TRUE THAT WE LOVE ONE ANOTHER

Words and Music by
Jack White

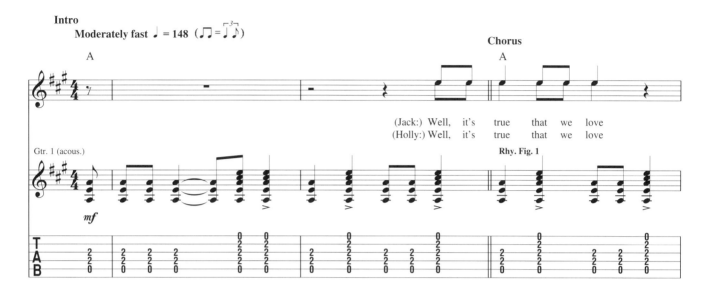

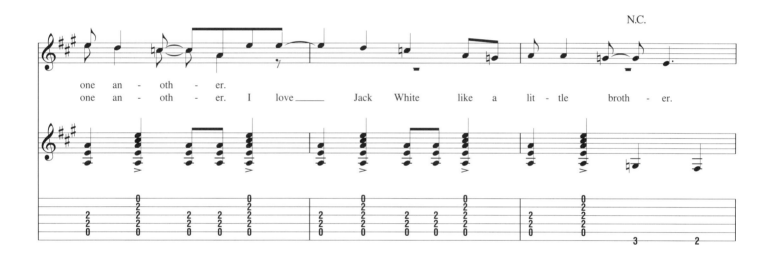

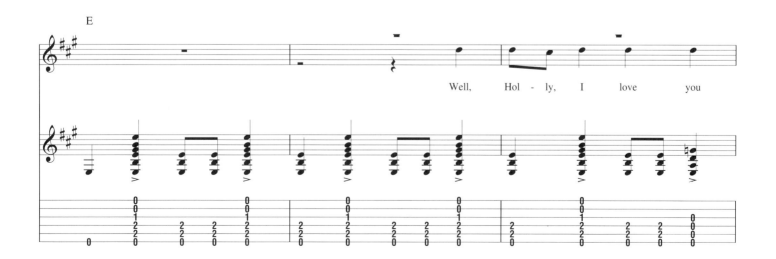

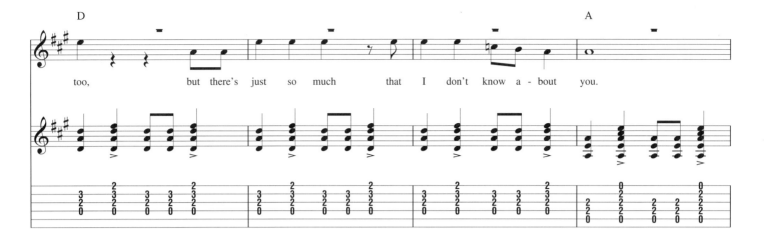

too, but there's just so much that I don't know a - bout you.

Verse

(Holly:) 1. Jack, give me some mon - ey to pay my bills.___

End Rhy. Fig. 1

(Jack:) All the

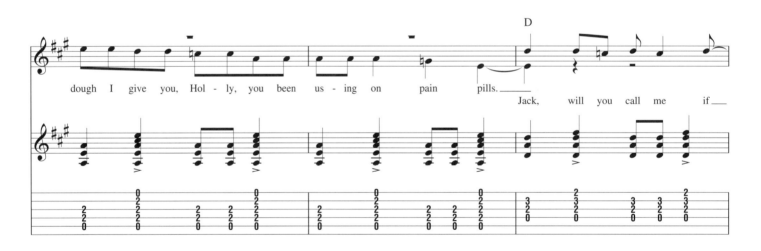

dough I give you, Hol - ly, you been us - ing on pain pills.___ Jack, will you call me if ___

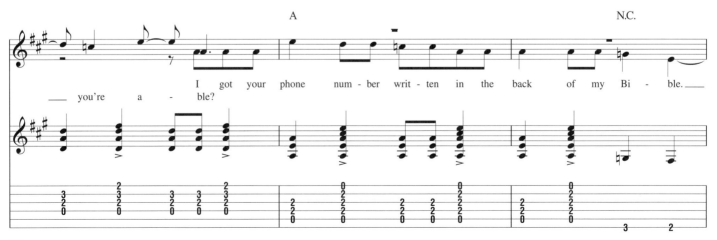

I got your phone num - ber writ - ten in the back of my Bi - ble.___

___ you're a - ble?

Verse

Gtr. 1: w/ Rhy. Fig. 1

(Meg:) 3. Just say "Jack, do you a - dore me?
(Jack:) Well, _____ I would, Hol - ly, but

(Holly:) Then I
love real - ly bores me. _____ Then I

guess we should just be friends.
guess we should just be friends. I'm just kid - ding, Hol - ly. You

know that I'll love you till the end.
(Jack:) Well, it's
(Holly:) Well, it's

Chorus

Gtr. 1: w/ Rhy. Fig. 1

true that we love one an - oth - er.
true that we love one an - oth - er. I love _____ Jack White like a

lit - tle broth - er.
Well,

Hol - ly, I love you too, but there's just so much that

I don't know a - bout you.
(Jack:) 4. Hol - ly,

Verse

Gtr. 1: w/ Rhy. Fig. 1 (1st 10 meas.)

give me some of your Eng - lish lov - in'.
(Holly:) If I did _____ that, Jack, _____ I'd have

one in the ov - en.
Why don't you

go off and love your-self?

If I did that, Hol - ly, there

won't be an - y - thing left for an - y - bod - y else.

Verse

Gtr. 1: w/ Rhy. Fig. 1 (1st 8 meas.)

(Holly:) 5. Jack, it's too bad a - bout the way that you look.

(Jack:)You know I

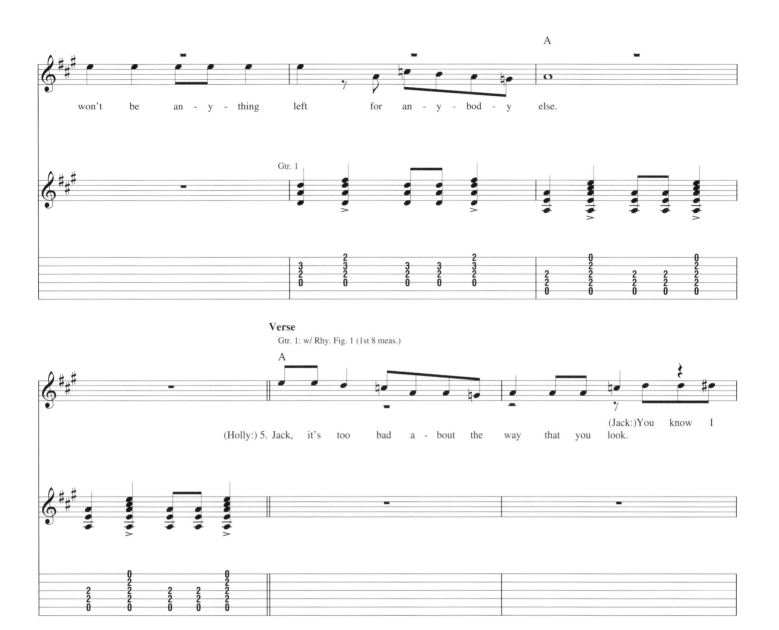

gave that horse a car - rot so he'd break your foot.

(Meg:) Will the two of you cut it out, _____ and

Guitar Notation Legend

Guitar Music can be notated three different ways: on a *musical staff*, in *tablature*, and in *rhythm slashes*.

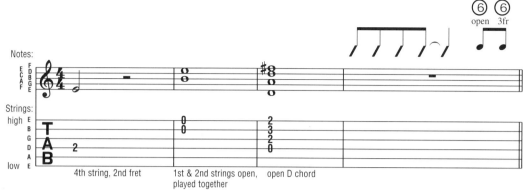

RHYTHM SLASHES are written above the staff. Strum chords in the rhythm indicated. Use the chord diagrams found at the top of the first page of the transcription for the appropriate chord voicings. Round noteheads indicate single notes.

THE MUSICAL STAFF shows pitches and rhythms and is divided by bar lines into measures. Pitches are named after the first seven letters of the alphabet.

TABLATURE graphically represents the guitar fingerboard. Each horizontal line represents a string, and each number represents a fret.

HALF-STEP BEND: Strike the note and bend up 1/2 step.

WHOLE-STEP BEND: Strike the note and bend up one step.

GRACE NOTE BEND: Strike the note and immediately bend up as indicated.

SLIGHT (MICROTONE) BEND: Strike the note and bend up 1/4 step.

BEND AND RELEASE: Strike the note and bend up as indicated, then release back to the original note. Only the first note is struck.

PRE-BEND: Bend the note as indicated, then strike it.

VIBRATO: The string is vibrated by rapidly bending and releasing the note with the fretting hand.

WIDE VIBRATO: The pitch is varied to a greater degree by vibrating with the fretting hand.

HAMMER-ON: Strike the first (lower) note with one finger, then sound the higher note (on the same string) with another finger by fretting it without picking.

PULL-OFF: Place both fingers on the notes to be sounded. Strike the first note and without picking, pull the finger off to sound the second (lower) note.

LEGATO SLIDE: Strike the first note and then slide the same fret-hand finger up or down to the second note. The second note is not struck.

SHIFT SLIDE: Same as legato slide, except the second note is struck.

TRILL: Very rapidly alternate between the notes indicated by continuously hammering on and pulling off.

TAPPING: Hammer ("tap") the fret indicated with the pick-hand index or middle finger and pull off to the note fretted by the fret hand.

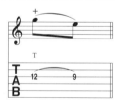

NATURAL HARMONIC: Strike the note while the fret-hand lightly touches the string directly over the fret indicated.

PINCH HARMONIC: The note is fretted normally and a harmonic is produced by adding the edge of the thumb or the tip of the index finger of the pick hand to the normal pick attack.

PICK SCRAPE: The edge of the pick is rubbed down (or up) the string, producing a scratchy sound.

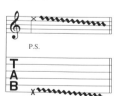

MUFFLED STRINGS: A percussive sound is produced by laying the fret hand across the string(s) without depressing, and striking them with the pick hand.

PALM MUTING: The note is partially muted by the pick hand lightly touching the string(s) just before the bridge.

RAKE: Drag the pick across the strings indicated with a single motion.

TREMOLO PICKING: The note is picked as rapidly and continuously as possible.

VIBRATO BAR DIVE AND RETURN: The pitch of the note or chord is dropped a specified number of steps (in rhythm) then returned to the original pitch.

VIBRATO BAR SCOOP: Depress the bar just before striking the note, then quickly release the bar.

VIBRATO BAR DIP: Strike the note and then immediately drop a specified number of steps, then release back to the original pitch.

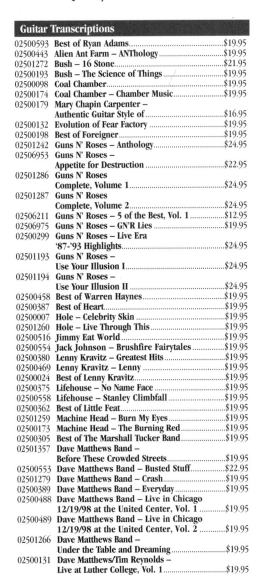

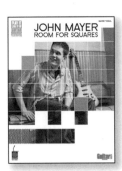